D0856368

Transforming the Curriculum for Multicultural Understandings:

A Practitioner's Handbook

James B. Boyer
Professor, Curriculum and American Ethnic Studies
College of Education
Kansas State University

and

H. Prentice Baptiste, Jr.
Professor, Foundations and Adult Education
Associate Director, Center for Science Education
Program Planner, Midwest Desegregation Assistance Center
College of Education
Kansas State University

Transforming the Curriculum
for Multicultural Understandings:
A Practitioner's Handbook

By James B. Boyer & H. Prentice Baptiste, Jr.

Copyright 1996 by James B. Boyer & H. Prentice Baptiste, Jr.

Published by Caddo Gap Press
   3145 Geary Boulevard, Suite 275
   San Francisco, California 94118

ISBN 1-880192-19-5

Price $19.95

       Library of Congress Cataloging-in-Publication Data

Boyer, James B.
   Transforming the curriculum for multicultural understandings : a
practitioner's handbook / James B. Boyer and H. Prentice Baptiste,
Jr.
      p.   cm.
   Includes bibliographical references (p.) and index.
   ISBN 1-880192-19-5 (alk. paper)
   1. Multicultural education--United States--Curricula--Handbooks,
manuals, etc. 2. Curriculum planning--United States--Handbooks,
manuals, etc. 3. Curriculum change--United States--Handbooks,
manuals, etc.   I. Baptiste, H. Prentice. II. Title.
LC1099.3.B48   1996
370.19'6'0973--dc20   96-30455
                                                             CIP

Contents

Chapter 6:
Baptiste's Typology of Multiculturalism 97

Chapter 7:
Moving the Environment toward Multiculturalism .. 129

...I do not want
my house to be
walled in on all sides
and my windows
to be stuffed.
I want the cultures
of all lands
to be blown
about my house
as freely as possible.
But I refuse
to be blown
off my feet by any.

—Mahatma Gandhi

Foreword

Over the past two decades, multicultural education has emerged as a serious discipline being studied by practitioners and scholars all over the world. The demographic realities of our time suggest that concepts of inclusion and cultural reflection are essential to any academic endeavor. This volume was undertaken with that consciousness, particularly as it relates to schooling in the United States, including the preparation of those who shall serve in instructional roles in schools. At the same time, we are well aware that all of America's major institutions are undergoing change and the delivery of services to all populations must now become somewhat more customized for maximum effectiveness.

As practitioners in the preparation and enhancement of those who teach as well as those in other human service roles, we offer this book in hopes that it will enlighthen and provide practical assistance in this multicultural society. We are both founding members of the National Association for Multicultural Education and feel that all those who share a commitment to diversity will embrace these ideas.

We are especially indebted to Edna and Lesley, our respective partners, whose association and insight added to the substantive impact of this volume. We are also indebted to Martha P. Scott for her untiring work with the original manuscript and creation of the index. Finally, our thanks to all the graduate students who shared and critiqued this work in its prepublication stages. It is our hope that you will find application to the diverse work already underway.

—*James B. Boyer & H. Prentice Baptiste, Jr.*
September 1996

We can, whenever
and wherever we choose,
successfully teach
all children whose schooling
is of interest to us.
We already know more than
we need, to successfully
teach all children.
Whether or not we do it
must finally depend on
how we feel about the fact
that we haven't so far.

—Ronald Edmonds

Introduction

In this introduction we present a rationale, purpose, and definition to support the transforming of a school's curriculum to a multicultural philosophy.

The reasons that today's professional practitioners of education and schooling must engage themselves in a commitment to multiculturalizing curriculum goes beyond changing demographics. In addition to changing demographics there are several other demanding reasons:

1. People as individuals and as group members are unwilling to be passive bystanders to such social institutions as schools, health providers, government entities, etc.

2. The demise of controlling centralizations, collective structures, and traditional institutions has brought about the emergence of a new individual and a new era of globalization featuring new technologies with accompanying empowerment of individuals.

3. The ebbing shifts of power globally, nationally, and regionally require a more ethical and equitable sharing of power if our species, *Homo sapiens*, is to survive.

4. The emergence of global cooperative-competitive paradigms in the marketplace requires a small margin of waste, involving a narrow tolerance or no tolerance at all of underutilization of human resources, and a high quality of cross-cultural human relations skills.

5. Our challenge has moved from the mechanistic challenge of the industrial and post-industrial eras, through the mass information of super communication highways, to an era requiring a moral, ethical, and equitable manner of relating cross-culturally.

Succinctly, the purpose of multiculturalizing education is the removal of the alienation attitude of education which confronts large numbers of students on a daily basis and to replace that alienation with a supported nurturing environment for all students. As Gay (1994) points out, the intent of education that is multicultural is not to destroy the unity of our country and its European cultural heritages. It is not the mere reducing of education to unsound pedagogical practices for the inclusion of people of color to make them feel good about themselves.

We see the concept of multiculturalizing as transforming education so that its reality for students includes equity for all, a true spirit of democracy, freedom from prejudice and stereotypes of discrimination, and appreciation for cultural diversity. It is to enable education as a cornerstone of society to align itself with a cultural pluralism philosophy that will enable us to make necessary major paradigm shifts that will allow all of our students to meet the challenges of the "new world order" of the 21st and 22nd centuries, each to become a truly global citizen.

It is projected that by the year 2020, 46 percent of the nation's student population will be students of color. Parenthetically, the twenty-five largest urban school districts in our country will have students of color populations in the majority. Correspondingly, the teacher population is becoming whiter. The teachers of color population has continued to shrink in spite of numerous efforts to reverse this trend.

A part of the purpose of multiculturalizing education is to facilitate cross-cultural communication, and to engender the evolution of a school environment which will nurture a positive respectful understanding among these diverse groups.

However, we would be remiss if we did not outline certain specific goals within the purpose of multiculturalizing education. These goals are:

1. An appreciation and respect for cultural diversity.

2. A promotion of understanding of unique cultural and ethnic heritages.

3. To promote the development of culturally responsible and responsive curriculum in all areas.

4. To facilitate the acquisition of the values, attitudes, skills, and knowledge to function beside and cooperatively with various cultures.

5. The reduction of racism and other "isms" in all areas of education as well as in our society.

6. The achievement of social, political, economic, and educational equity for **all** students.

We turn now to the challenge of defining multicultural education or multiculturalizing education. Our combined experiences with the concept (multicultural) are in excess of fifty years. If nothing else, this lifelong set of experiences has taught us that defining the concept multicultural—and its derivations: multicultural education, education that is multicultural, multiculturalism, multiculturalizing education—is a complex undertaking.

Fortunately or unfortunately, the concept has internalized an evolving dynamicism as scholars tend to operationalize its theoretical and descriptive constraints. The spectrum of theoretical constructs ranges from Sizemore's (1980) construct of multicultural as a political concept to Baptiste's (1980) construct of multicultural as a philosophical concept. Other writers have placed the emphasis of the construct on human relations

(Colangelo, Dustin, & Foxley, 1985), group differences (Cross, Baker, & Stiles, 1977), an ideology of cultural pluralism (Bennett, 1990), a reform movement (Banks & Banks, 1989), constructive social, political, and educational equity (Ramsey, Vold, & Williams, 1989), individuals who can operate in two or more cultures (Gollnick & Chinn, 1994), and school program-appropriate experiences for diverse students (Baruth & Manning, 1992).

A definition of multiculturalizing education which we found to be comprehensive and encompassing of the rationale and purpose as previously presented is Suzuki's definition:

> Multicultural education is an educational program which provides multiple learning environments that properly match the academic and social needs of the students. These needs may vary widely due to differences in the race, sex, ethnicity, or social class background of the students. In addition to developing their basic academic skills, the program should help students develop a better understanding of their own backgrounds and other groups that compose our society. Thorough this process, the program should help students to respect and appreciate cultural diversity, overcome ethnocentric and prejudicial attitudes, and understand the sociocultural, economic, and psychological factors that have produced the contemporary conditions of ethnic polarization, inequality, and alienation. It should also foster their ability to critically analyze and make intelligent decisions about real-life problems and issues through a process of democratic, dialogical inquiry. Finally, it should help them conceptualize and aspire toward a vision of a better society and acquire the necessary knowledge, understandings, skills to enable them to move the society toward greater equality and freedom, the eradication of degrading poverty and dehumanizing dependency, and the development of meaningful identity for all people.
> —Bob Suzuki, "Multicultural Education: What's it all about?" *Integrated Education*, 1979

However, for the purpose of this handbook, the authors are offering the following definition of multicultural education:

Multicultural Education is a comprehensive philosophical reform of the school environment essentially focused on the principles of equity, success, and social justice for all students. Equity is the result of changing the school environment, especially the curriculum and instruction component, through restructuring and reorganization so that students from diverse racial, ethnic, and social classes experience educational equality and cultural empowerment. Success is demonstrated through parity representation of achievement of the school or district's students across racial, ethnic, cultural, and social classes. Social justice in schools is accomplished by the process of judicious pedagogy as its cornerstone and focuses on unabridged knowledge, reflection, and social action as the foundation for social change.

—Baptiste, 1995

In addition to a spectrum of definitions on the concept of multicultural, there has been an analysis of the concept by the following writers: Baptiste, Baptiste, & Gollnick, 1980; Boyer, 1985; Banks & Banks, 1989; and Sleeter & Grant, 1988. These writers have provided typologies for classifying the concept into several categories or levels which differ both quantitatively and qualitatively. We will revisit Baptiste's typology in Chapter Six.

References Cited

Banks, J. & Banks, C. (1989). *Multicultural education: Issues & perspectives*. Boston, MA: Allyn & Bacon.

Baptiste, Jr., H.P., Baptiste, M.L., & Gollnick, D.M. (1980). *Multicultural teacher education: Preparing educators to provide educationl equity,* Vol. 1. Washington, DC: American Association of Colleges for Teacher Education.

Baptiste, Jr., H.P. (1995). Definition of multicultural education. Proposed comprehensive remedial plan and order for the Rockford School District. Rockford, IL.

Baptiste, M. & Baptiste, Jr., H.P. (1980). *Competencies toward multiculturalism in multicultural teacher education: Preparing educators to provide education equity*, Vol. 1. Washington, DC: American Association of Colleges for Teacher Education.

Baruth, L.G. & Manning, M.L. (1992). *Multicultural education of children and adolescents*. Needham Heights, MA: Allyn & Bacon.

Bennett, C. (1990). *Comprehensive multicultural education: Theory and practice,* 2nd edition. Boston, MA: Allyn & Bacon.

Boyer, J.B. (1985). *Multicultural education: Product or process* (Reprinted 1991). New York: Eric Center on Urban Education, Teachers College, Columbia University (Now available through the College of Education, Kansas State University).

Colangelo, N., Dustin, D., & Foxley, C. (1985). *Multicultural nonsexist education: A human relations approach*. Dubuque, IA: Kendall Hunt.

Cross, D., Baker, G., & Stiles, L. (1977). *Teaching in a multicultural society: Perspectives and professional strategies*. New York: Free Press.

Gay, G. (1994). *At the essence of learning: Multicultural education*. West Lafayette, IN: Kappa Delta Pi.

Gollnick, D. & Chinn, P.C. (1994). *Multicultural education in a pluralistic society,* 4th edition. Columbus, OH: MacMillan.

Ramsey, P.G., Vold, E.B., & Williams, L.R. (1989). *Multicultural education: A Resource book*. New York: Garland.

Sizemore, B. (1980). The politics of multicultural education. Unpublished manuscript.

Sleeter, C.E. & Grant, C.A. (1988). *Making choices for multicultural education: Five approaches to race, class, and gender*. Columbus, OH: Merrill.

Suzuki, B.H. (1979). Multicultural education: What's it all about? *Integrated Education,* 17, 43-49.

Notes

What we give
to children
(learners)—
they will give
back to society.

—Karl Menninger

Chapter 1

Rationale for a Multicultural Curriculum

Elements of the Transformation of the Curriculum

Of the thousands of school superintendents, principals, curriculum directors, associates, teachers, and support staff who work in schools daily, most are genuinely interested in the continuous development of the school's program. Yet, it is well known that the schools are one of America's favorite targets for criticism. Overall, more than five million persons work daily in the schools or in school-related services. Given this tremendous investment from the workforce, our position is that the school's program—the curriculum—is the lifeblood of the American way of life.

There is no denying its significance in the literacy development of a nation that bases its existence on a functioning democracy, on implementation of democratic principles. There can be no sustaining of the freedoms now enjoyed in the United States without sustaining a curriculum that socializes learners to their role and responsibilities in the human intellectual enterprise.

The Curriculum—the School's Program

For several centuries, Americans have supported their schools financially and have charged each state with exercising the powers to insure that schools exist to serve their learners. That charge includes intellectual development as well as moral orientation.

In 1635, the Boston Latin Grammar School established the framework of the curriculum employed today in many schools. While it seemed appropriate at the time, one must remember that one of the objectives of that curriculum was to provide a program "for boys from upper income families." Subsequently, when the student population changed, few efforts were made to better align the curriculum with those who would come to consume such a program and who were not boys from upper income families. More recently, thousands of school workers (administrators, teachers, and support personnel) have come to realize that the traditional curriculum does not serve all populations very well—that it is in need of transformation.

As the demographics of America change, so must programmatic emphasis. There remains a clear commitment to the traditional objectives of the American curriculum: one must accomplish the skills of reading, writing, computing, and relating to other human beings. The multicultural transformation of the curriculum suggests further that the program's framework must change toward the goal of becoming more inclusive and more psychologically accommodating, and the elements for such transformation must begin with the perspectives of those who work in schools as well as those who make policy and financially support schools.

What about Those Schools Whose Demographics Have Not Changed Dramatically at This Time? Why Should Their Curriculum Upgrade Itself?

It is understood that many rural and suburban schools in America are not yet experiencing the same racial and ethnic changes in their student populations as some other locations. First, this does not mean that such changes are soon to occur (although they may well be). Secondly, if there is no diversity in the student population, then it is incumbent upon curriculum workers to provide curriculum experiences which shape the thinking of their student populations toward equity and diversity, because overall America is changing, and students from any area—rural, urban, or whatever—must be prepared in their education to cope with such changes.

It would be rare to find a school, a teacher, or a school district that does not want to educate its students for a society that must embrace change and cope with change. Part of the change is a new understanding of the power and impact of curriculum content, instructional style and expertise, and the entire academic socialization process for learners in American schools.

For Further Thought

1. Given the brief history of multicultural understandings and public education in the United States, which aspect helps you most to understand some of the concerns educators and others have about multicultural education today?

2. Is multicultural education different from multicultural currriculum?

3. What is meant by diversity?

4. Develop your own definition of multicultural education? What are the basic tenets of your definition?

Notes

Knowledge
is socially
distributed...what
you know is what
you have been
allowed to know.

—H. Prentice
Baptiste, Jr.

Chapter 2

Historical Look at the Emergence of Diversity in the American Curriculum

Historical Perspective

A definitive clarification of multicultural education lies in a socio-historical look at our society. The national society of our country has been examined and analyzed from a sociological perspective on several occasions. Each of these analyses dealt with the various kinds of people—that is, the diversity of groups that constituted the population of this country. A few sociologists, such as Gunnar Myrdal (1962) and Talcott Parsons (1965), presented explanations of the interactive relationship among the various cultural, racial, and ethnic groups.

The three sociological concepts that have primarily been utilized to explain the interactive relationship among the various social, racial, cultural, and ethnic groups are Americanization, the melting pot, and cultural pluralism. These concepts are dissimilar in their intent for members of various social groups.

The Americanization Concept

The proponents of the Americanization process during the late 1800s and early 1900s were concerned about the influx of more than twenty million Eastern and Southern European immigrants to the United States. These immigrants were not only viewed as poor, but also of culturally and racially inferior stock. Cubberly, a distinguished education leader, in his book *Changing Conception of Education* (1909), wrote:

> the southern and eastern Europeans are a very different type from the north Europeans, who preceded them. Illiterate, docile, lacking in self-reliance and initiative, and possessing none of the Anglo-Teutonic conceptions of law, order, and government, their coming has served to dilute tremendously our national stock, and to corrupt our civic life....
>
> Our task is to break up their groups or settlements, to assimilate and to amalgamate these people as part of our American race, and to implant in their children, so far as can be done, the Anglo-Saxon conceptions of righteousness, law and order, and popular government, and to awaken in them reverence for our democratic institutions and for those things in our national life which we as people hold to be of abiding worth.

Cubberly's stature in the educational community lead to an unquestionable acceptance of his ideas and beliefs. Educational systems operationalized his philosophy in an assimilation process of immigrants' children, which deprived them of their cultural heritage as they were Americanized.

This process did not leave out their parents. President Theodore Roosevelt (1910) shared the xenophobic views of Cubberly and utilized his political influence to enhance the

Americanization process. He denounced the idea of hyphenated Americans—Irish-Americans, Polish-Americans, and so on; this approach he considered to be disloyal to the country because he perceived it as holding allegiance both to America and to something else. His uncompromising position coerced many immigrants to forsake their heritage, their roots, for the new and "better" life. The Americanization phenomenon was an assimilation process of Anglo-Saxon cultural imperialism.

The Melting Pot

The melting pot theory was not synonymous with the Americanization process. The objectives of these two concepts were distinctly different. Promotion of Nordic Anglo-Saxon superiority in all aspects of life, along with promotion of the inherent inferiority of non-Nordic origins of life, was the essence of the Americanization process.

On the other hand, the melting pot theory proposed that a new "hybrid" group would emerge from the various distinct sociocultural groups. The *sine qua non* of this theory was that all groups would contribute on a parity basis to the production of a unique and superior American race. However, the mutual mixing of the diverse groups in this country was not allowed to occur, and thus did not take place. Subsequently, we had the myth of the melting pot. As stated by Pratte (1979, p. 29):

When a metaphor is no longer believed to be an "as if" vehicle for organizing our thinking and is taken to be a literal statement, a myth has been born.

It was in the early 1900s when this myth received its greatest impetus. The Broadway play entitled *The Melting Pot*, by Israel Zangwill (1922), transformed the ideal to a myth by implying this amal-gamation was a fact of American life, not an ideal by which we might judge our attempts to achieve a very difficult goal.

Cultural Pluralism

The concept of cultural pluralism is not new. However, of the three, it is possibly the least understood. One of its most able proponents—Horace Kallen—met with fierce opposition when he presented his theory of cultural pluralism as an ideal sociological model for our society. He believed that the various cultural groups of our society could maintain their identity while coexisting in a mutually supportive system. He argued that cultural pluralism did not necessarily lead to disunity.

Kallen's conception of cultural pluralism did not mean that our country would become a "mosaic of cultures." He stated in the early 1920s that there was a mainstream American culture that was historically not monolithic but pluralistic. Kallen believed that this pluralism had its roots in the founding of America, its basic political documents (the *Declaration of Independence* and the *Constitution*), the frontier tradition, the way in which the American people settled on this continent, and the values they developed. He believed cultural pluralism was intrinsic to what he called "the American idea."

In his book, *Cultural Pluralism and the American Idea*, Kallen (1956) presented his version of Americanization. Kallen wrote that Americanization means the acceptance by all Americans, native and foreign born, of "an over-arching culture based on the 'American idea.'" This overarching American culture is pluralistic because it reflects a pluralistic society. Pluralism is the essence of its strength and attraction. Kallen believed that cultures

> live and grow in and through the individual, and their vitality is a function of individual diversities of interests and associations. Pluralism is the *sine qua non* of their persistence and prosperous growth.

A Comparative Analysis

The previously discussed sociological concepts had their strong proponents and followers during the early part of the 20th century. It is of interest that the real winner—Americanism—was never publicly attested to by the masses, that the alleged winner—melting pot—was a psychological myth, and that the loser—cultural pluralism—has since reemerged. Furthermore, each of the sociological concepts—Americanism, melting pot, and cultural pluralism—promoted during the early 20th century explicitly or implicitly supported racism. Each concept was politically motivated, and the public school system had a role in the operationalizing or nonoperationalizing of the concepts.

The hindsight of contemporary history allows us to realize that the Americanization process as proposed by Cubberly and others became the *modus operandi* for the socialization of inhabitants of the United States. Our institutions—public school, government entities, and so on—exuded copiously the values and attitudes of Anglo-Americans to the detriment of any other group's values and attitudes. The Anglicization of non-Anglo names, life-styles, family practices, speech patterns, and so on, surreptitiously became the order of the times. In spite of the ideal society as presented in Zangwill's play *The Melting Pot*, which found strong support in the masses of Americans, the real winner with respect to the accepted values, lifestyles, and social practices of the nation was Americanism.

It may come as a surprise to some that none of these sociological concepts was devoid of racism. Proponents of the melting pot theory did not intend for the amalgamation or melting process to include people of color or any visible ethnics. Actually, African Americans, Asian Americans, Native Americans, and Mexican Americans, although very numerous in the United States during the turn of the century, were not included in the theories of Americanization, melting pot, and cultural pluralism. The focus of each of these conceptual theories was those immigrants from Southern and Eastern Europe. It was not the intent of these theories to provide any equitable relationship between people of color and white people. Therefore, each theory had a definite racist nature.

This is a political society. The basis of its operation is majority rule within a political democracy. Paramount to this political democracy is the inequitable distribution of goods, values, status, and power. Because politics is the management of conflict that results when different groups are in dispute over scarce resources, power, and status, an identification of the opposing groups must be made, and an interpretation of their stakes and stands must be given (Sizemore, 1980). The Americanization idea explicitly stated its political position as Krug (1976, pp. 12-13) describes Fairchild's argument in this way:

> While the racial makeup of the American people would be hard to define, an American nationality did exist, based on Nordic or Anglo-Saxon cultural values and mores. The American nation, according to Fairchild, was formed principally by immigrants from England, Ireland, Germany, and the Scandinavian countries. But "beginning about 1882," he wrote, "the immigration problem in the United States has become increasingly a racial problem in two distinct ways: first by altering profoundly the Nordic predominance in the American population, and second by introducing various new elements which are so different from any of the old ingredients that even small quantities are deeply significant." These "new elements" consisted of Italians, Poles, and Jews, who were coming to the United States in large numbers. "The American People," Fairchild argued, "have since the revolution resisted any threat of dilution by a widely different race and must continue to do so in the case of large-scale immigration. If they fail to do so, the

American nation would face the beginning of the process of mongrelization."

The "melting pot" idea, according to Fairchild, was "slowly, insidiously, irresistibly eating away the very heart of the United States. What was being melted in the great Melting Pot, losing all form and symmetry, all beauty and character, and nobility and usefulness, was the American nationality itself."

What the immigrants had to be told, with great kindness and full consideration, according to Fairchild, was that they were welcome to the United States under the condition that they would renounce their respective cultural values and embrace the dominant culture forged by the predominantly Nordic American people since its independence. The American public schools must be made the effective tools of achieving this objective, at least as far as the children of the immigrants were concerned, and this process must be accomplished as far as possible.

Neither the melting pot nor the cultural pluralism theorists provided clear explanations for dealing with the political context of our society. Their single-minded focus on the "amalgamation" or "unity in diversity" of the various white cultural/ethnic groups blinded them to the reality of the political obstacles that stood in the way of such noble endeavors. As Pratte pointed out:

The melting pot ideology made two assumptions: first, that immigrant groups in American society were unwilling to pay the price of Americanization and did not want to "make it" on WASP terms; second, that the American culture was accepting and tolerant of "foreign ways" to allow for the fusion and emergence of a "new American." (Pratte, 1979)

Basically, each assumption was faulty. Kallen maintained that the majority culture would benefit from the coexistence and constant interaction with the various cultural/ethnic groups; whereas, the various cultural/ethnic groups would accept and cherish the "common" elements of American cultural, political, and social mores as represented by the public schools, through their own efforts he believed they would also support supplemental education for their children to preserve their ethnic cultural awareness and values. Kallen's theory failed to consider the intolerant attitude of the Americanists and the willingness of the immigrant groups to forsake their cultural and ethnic heritage. Kallen's theory of cultural pluralism ignored, to its detriment, the political nature of our society.

Rediscovery of Cultural Pluralism

Surely scholars writing in 2100 will have a clearer perspective as to what lead to a broader acceptance of the ideal of cultural pluralism during the 1990s. Nevertheless, without the benefit of their time lag, we would like briefly to submit our reasons for the rediscovery of cultural pluralism. It has become obvious to many Americans that Americanization was a denigrating, ethnocentric process, which forced many individuals to scoff at or reject their heritage. Also, numerous publications had led to the renouncement of the melting pot theory as a myth (Novak, 1973). These observations paved the way for the acceptance of cultural pluralism via the demise of the Americanization process and the melting pot theory.

However, certain proactive actions—such as: (a) the emergence of self-determination by minority ethnic groups; (b) the *Brown v. Board of Education* Supreme Court decision of 1954; (c) civil rights legislation; (d) the emergence of ethnicity; (e) the impact of mass media; and (f) the sociopolitical climate of our country—led to the rediscovery of the cultural pluralism ideal as a viable alternative philosophical goal governing the interrelationship of the various cultural/ethnic groups within our country.

In his publication, *The Rise of the Unmeltable Ethnics*, Novak (1973) presents an eloquent case for White ethnic groups who failed to melt and who also rejected the Americanization process. These groups have maintained their ethnicity. They believed that being a hyphenated American is perfectly all right. Actually, they will argue that being an American is being the composite product of several cultures. The intense resurgence of ethnicity by numerous groups—Afro-Americans, Polish Americans, Italian Americans, and so on—during the 1970s led several writers to refer to it as the decade of the ethnics.

The mass media, especially television, has been a significant catalyst in the resurgence of cultural pluralism. The consciousness of Americans was raised via the television exposure of Martin Luther King, Jr.'s marches for freedom, segregationists taunting African American students entering Little Rock High School, Jewish Americans being taunted in Cicero, and programs such as *Roots* and *Holocaust*. These and many other televised examples of racism, ethnocentrism, discrimination, and other forms of dehumanization served a significant function in the recognition and acceptance of all groups. There is no question about the sociopolitical climate of our society being more receptive of cultural pluralism during this time than any other time in our history.

The concept of cultural pluralism that emerged in the 1960s was not the same as the one espoused by Kallen in the early 1900s. Nor was the impetus the same. Furthermore, the ambiguity of the 1960s concept has been greater. The ambiguity of the concept has been extensively discussed in the writings of Pratte (1979), Green (1966), and Pacheco (1977). Each of these writers agrees that cultural pluralism refers to a theory of society; however, the often-raised question is "should the theory be viewed as descriptive or prescriptive?" Our response is that it is both. It has also been stated that there are different conceptual theories of cultural pluralism. Several that have recently appeared in the literature are democratic pluralism, insular pluralism, modified pluralism, and open society.

Democratic pluralism is descriptive. It refers to a concept of cultural pluralism in which there is a balance of power between competing and overlapping religious, cultural, ethnic, economic, and geographical groupings. Pacheco (1977, p. 18) states:

> each group has some interests which it protects and fosters and each has some say in shaping social decisions which are all binding on all groups that make up the society. Common to all groups is a set of political values and beliefs which serve to maintain the entire social system through accommodation and resolution to conflicts via appropriate channels.

This description has largely been accepted as the form of political organization that exists in our society.

Insular pluralism is descriptive of the relationships among various social groups. The subgroups of the society as much as possible live in isolation from one another. Each group places restrictions on the amount and kind of associations its members may have with outsiders. As Green (1966) and Pratte (1979) have pointed out in separate writings, the various social groups will allow their members to develop primary and secondary relationships within their respective groups; however, intergroup associations and relationships may exist only at the level of polity. Although this form of cultural pluralism professes a respect and recognition of cultural diversity within society, it is very restrictive of each individual. The individual is confined to the social and cultural confines of his or her cultural group regardless of the wishes of the individual. Thus, insular pluralism allows each group to maintain its community and culture while supporting the social value of freedom of association for groups, but not for individuals.

The modified or halfway pluralism is not too different from

insular pluralism; however, it encourages a high degree of functional contact between members of various cultural groups at the level of secondary associations. Pratte's (1979) criticism of this form of cultural pluralism is as follows:

> The fundamental difficulty inherent in the dynamics of the model of halfway pluralism is that the increased contact among groups on the secondary level of association may and often does promote cultural assimilation. (p. 129)

Pratte fails to acknowledge the possibility of acculturation. In cultural acculturation, the individuals retain and maintain their primary cultural heritage and experience while acquiring the skills and knowledge of another or other cultures. Thus, the individuals are able to function effectively in their primary culture and other cultures also. The faultiness of Pratte's reasoning lies in his belief that primary and secondary associations of members from various cultures can only culminate in an assimilation process. His writings imply that an individual can only function in one culture and that in order to function in another cultural setting one will lose the ability to function in one's primary culture.

Banks's (1977) typology model on ethnicity addresses the hypothesis that an individual may function effectively in two or more cultures; however, more important, Banks's typology opens the door for the exploration of ways for facilitating the acculturation process. Some research utilizing Banks's model lends support to the acculturation process (Ford, 1979).

The concept of cultural pluralism as an open society appears both descriptive and prescriptive. However, there is confusion because some observers believe our society is moving toward an open society and, therefore, away from cultural pluralism. One such observer, Green (1966), believes that an open society is one in which cultural groups and differences are irrelevant and eliminated. This has an apparent similarity to Talcott Parsons's prediction of the disappearance of ethnic groups from American society during the 20th century. Green's assertion that we are moving toward an open society in the United States is highly questionable, when on examination one realizes his concept of an open society eliminates the significance of cultural groups, much less the reality of their present and future existence.

In the Association for Supervision and Curriculum Development (ASCD) 1974 yearbook (Della-Dora, 1974), we are introduced to another definition of an open society. This definition includes the very essence of cultural pluralism because it is descriptive and prescriptive. It describes an

> open society in which a variety of cultures, value systems, and life styles not only coexist but are nurtured.... The major concern of the society at large, and of the schools in particular, would be for full participation of all human beings with rights which are not dependent on race, ethnicity, sex, or social class. Individual and group differences would be prized, not merely accepted or grudgingly tolerated, and every person would have equal access to what they want from and can give to the society. (p. 3)

ASCD's open society concept of cultural pluralism is relevant to the contemporary meaning and philosophical intent of cultural pluralism. This concept of cultural pluralism is both descriptive and prescriptive. It is descriptive in that it recognizes the real social structure of this society, that is, the existence of cultural diversity as evident by the various cultural ethnic groups and their relationship to certain national institutions and value systems of this country.

It is prescriptive because it dares to say what ought to be. That is, cultural diversity should not only be recognized but also valued at both the group and personal levels; that not only is equitable treatment received by all, but equitable accessibility provided to all with associated societal rights and privileges.

Cultural Pluralism to Multiculturalism

The concept of cultural pluralism led to the emergence of multiculturalism. Multiculturalism refers to a process of education that affiliates itself not only with the descriptive nature but, more important, to the prescriptive nature of cultural pluralism. This prescriptive nature of cultural pluralism is manifested in numerous statements and definitions of multiculturalism (multicultural education) as illustrated in the following definition:

> Multiculturalism should help students develop a better understanding of their own backgrounds and of other groups that compose our society. Through this process the program should help students to respect and appreciate cultural diversity, overcome ethnocentric and prejudicial attitude, and understand the socio-historical, economic, and psychological factors that have produced the contemporary conditions of ethnic polarization, inequality, and alienation. It should also foster their ability to critically analyze and make intelligent decisions about real-life problems and issues through a process of democratic, dialogical inquiry. Finally, it should help them conceptualize and aspire toward a vision of a better society and acquire the necessary knowledge, understanding, and skills to enable them to move society toward greater equality and freedom, the eradication of degrading poverty and dehumanizing dependency, and the development of meaningful identity for all people. (Suzuki, 1979, pp. 47-48)

Common to definitions and statements of multiculturalism is what should or ought to be and the implicitness of their relationship to the development of an ideal society. Therefore, education that is truly reflective of cultural pluralism will be guided by the prescriptive statement of multiculturalism. Thus, the purpose of multiculturalism becomes that of ascertaining the ideal culturally pluralistic society. Unfortunately, that has not been the case. A brief exploration of the 1960s sociological direction will give ample evidence to support our identifying this as a "blaming the victim" position.

The Sociology of "Blaming the Victim"

In spite of the 1954 Supreme Court decision *(Brown v. Board of Education)*, the sociology of the 1950s and 1960s did not support equity educational programs for all students. As a matter of fact, the sociology of this period presented a repertoire of studies to rationalize inequality.

The noted leaders of this racist and oppressive sociology were in particular: James Coleman, *Equality of Educational Opportunity* (1966); Daniel Patrick Moynihan, "Benign Neglect" (1965); Arthur Jensen, *How Much Can We Boost IQ and Scholastic Achievement?* (1969); and C.S. Jencks, *Inequality: A Reassessment of the Effect of Family and Schooling in America* (1972).

In his study *Equality of Educational Opportunity*, Coleman reported the following: African American students had access to educational resources that were very nearly equal to the resources that white students had, thus making our schools seem more equal than they were thought to be at that time. However, African American students scored substantially below white students. He further reported that affluent students performed much better than poor students. The significance of Coleman's report is that it let schools off the hook—that is, schools were blameless for the nonperformance of African American and poor children.

Moynihan stated that benign neglect was the best our society could do. Moynihan argued that the poor are characterized by intrinsic disabilities that account for their low standing in our social order. He further argued that school reform is wasted on the poor, since only massive intervention in the life of the poor would eliminate the intrinsic disabilities from which they suffer.

Jensen and his followers (Shockley, Banzield, Hernstein), utilizing the pseudoscience of IQ with the trickery of statistical manipulations, raised the old nurture-nature debate of learning disability. Jensen argued that the failure of recent compensatory efforts to produce lasting effects on children's IQs and achievement suggest that the premises on which these efforts have been based should be reexamined. Jensen did not mean that the ethnocentric value system that gave rise to compensatory education should be examined. Nor did he mean that the racist process of forcing African American and poor children to fit the cultural mold of middle-class Anglo children should be examined. He was raising the age-old argument: which contributed more to IQ development—genetics or environment?

Jensen buttressed his case for IQ development being heavily determined by genetics on Burt's twin studies. Recently, Burt's twin studies have been severely questioned and possibly represent the most blatant scientific farce of the 20th century (Gillie, 1977). It appears that Burt fabricated the studies and "cited collaborators" to further his own ideas of White supremacy. Thus, the cornerstone of Jensen's "genetic determination argument" has been unceremoniously removed.

Jencks's study, *Inequality*, gave wide support to those sociological parameters of "blaming the victim" for their ills. He promoted the causal relationship between being poor, minority status, coming from a broken home, seemingly low intelligence, and low school achievement. A critical analysis of the works of Coleman, Moynihan, Jensen, Jencks, and others will lead one to the conclusion that all statistical weapons were being aimed at the victim.

A Sociology of Equity Education

It was not until the 1970s that other sociological premises, questions, and perspectives regarding the education of African American, poor, and urban youth began to be systematically investigated. This sociological inquiry has focused on the process of schooling. This new inquiry removes the burden of responsibility from the victim and places it where it rightfully belongs— on the educational system.

Besides the legal dismantling via *Brown v. Board of Education*, one must not overlook the impact of student protests on overturning the segregated school system. Student protests, however, focused on much more than the need for non-segregated schooling. African American students (high school and college) also protested the curriculum's exclusion of Black History. Thus began a series of challenges to the American curriculum which is still underway. It has resulted in the following considerations:

1. Courses made available as electives in both the secondary school and in colleges.

An elective course remains an optional experience for most students and, though it is valuable, it does not necessarily become an institutionalized learning experience. It is entirely up to the student's choice, and then only if he or she hears about its existence. An elective course does not have the same impact on institutional transformation as does a required course or experience.

2. Courses made available as requirements in schools.

A required course becomes a necessary experience for each learner in a given program and, as such, has been deemed an essential experience. Program planners have endorsed the experience of such course as one which enriches, prepares, and elevates the thinking or skills of all those who enroll. At this point in our academic history, few programs require courses for understanding equity or for ethnic literacy for all those who enroll.

3. Expansions of equal opportunities for economically poor populations.

Following some major national legislation during the 1960s, America became more aware of its institutional and programmatic responsibilities to all of its children, all of its citizens—including the economically poor. Such expansion called for courses, experiences, and programs devoted to inclusion of this population and devoted to the institutionalization of concerns of strong interest to them. Additionally, this expansion generated new research and new literature and America began its debate on what is most appropriate for economically poor populations in schools as well as other agencies.

4. Programming for persons who do not have English as a first language (bilingual programming).

Because more than thirty million Americans have some language other than English as their first language, those institutions and curriculum programs that sought to be fair, equitable, inclusive, and culturally responsive began initiating bilingual education services and instruction in English as a second language. Fewer than five percent of all American teachers can speak more than one language, but many are skilled in the research regarding the skills for second language acquisition. The provisions of academic services to persons whose first language is something other than English implies that the educational program is attempting to develop an inclusive image and characteristic which is consistent with a quest for equity.

5. Accessibility of facilities and programming for persons with handicapping conditions.

Just a few years ago there were few ramps for persons confined to wheelchairs and there were no parking spaces reserved near building entrances for the physically challenged. America's movement in this direction is an example of societal transformation to accommodate all of its citizens. The Education for All Exceptional Persons Act (1965) and the Americans with Disabilities Act (1991) both gave major impetus for upgrading academic programs and facilities.

6. Greater inclusion of both genders (male and female) in curriculum programming and the workplace. (Elimination of discrimination based on gender).

American education categorically excluded information about females for generations and some of the information (and images) passed on about males actually distorted masculinity and social roles. With the increased awareness of how images and information can restrict opportunities or expand opportunities, programs of Women's Studies, Gender Equity, and Men's Studies have emerged. Few up-to-date curriculum programs would attempt to exclude such concerns as we approach the year 2000.

7. Categorical denial of policies, programs, and procedures which serve to discriminate on the basis of race, creed, color, gender, age, language or handicapping condition.

Over the last two decades, new levels of analyses have been underway as policies were reviewed that impact all persons involved in any institutional program. Policies reflect the perspectives of those who create policy and the limited profiles on many policy-making boards have resulted in policies that seemed inclusive, but frequently fell short in many ways. This new analyses attempts to raise consciousness and accommodate all.

The above list is not necessarily complete, but it offers a framework for what happened in two decades of American life, thereby providing the foundation for the transformation of which we speak. Curriculum in America was impacted by all of the above societal and institutional changes. However, very little has occurred in the school curriculum that goes directly to the heart of why many Americans are now calling for curriculum transformation. In order to have a society continue its way of life and have its members participate individually in decisions affecting their own lives, literacy must be at the core of our socialization. The schools have been charged with maintaining such literacy—and thus such a way of life.

A major element of such transformation is the perspective of those who work daily in curriculum activity as well as those who support direct instruction.

Legislation Of The 1960s and 1970s Impacting Diversity

The following pieces of national legislation in the decades of the 1960s and 1970s impacted the curriculum, and almost all of these laws have had implications or directives for the aforementioned transformation. The transformation, it should be remembered, would result in a pluralizing of the curriculum.

There is a quest for a more inclusive, more diverse, more functional learning program which respects the presence of the major profiles of the American citizenry. While there are numerous profiles, much of the beginning efforts must address the populations which were historically omitted from formal learning. These populations include (but are not limited to) the Native American learner, the African American learner, the Hispanic learner, the Asian learner, the Biracial learner, the learner for whom English is not a first language, the female learner as well as the male learner, the economically poor learner, and the learner who may be experiencing a handicapping condition.

The Civil Rights Act, 1964

This national legislation was considered a landmark in America's quest for accommodating all of its citizens without discrimination. It provided for access to public facilities for all Americans and it prohibited discrimination in any form based on race, color, creed, religion, or national origin.

The Economic Opportunity Act, 1964

This legislation attempted to respond to America's war on poverty and included provisions for the first Headstart Programs to serve preschool children from impoverished families, among over provisions.

The Elementary-Secondary Education Act, 1965

This was considered, at the time, the most comprehensive national legislation devoted to education below the post-secondary level and it included extending the kind of services provided in early childhood to elementary schooling as well as enriching school programs like libraries. It also included the provision for acquiring new equipment for instruction.

The Voting Rights Act, 1965

Understanding that the preservation of a democracy involves the participation of all the people in governing their lives, Congress, with much controversy, passed this legislation to ensure that no one would be prohibited from participating as an American voter if they were eligible. The privilege of voting allows a citizen to exercise one's right to participate in choosing the leaders as well as creating policies and setting procedures. Political sophistication is essential to an equitable society.

The Bilingual Education Act, 1968

This legislation attempted to indicate that instructional services should recognize the first language of the learner and, in the transition to an English-speaking curriculum, children should be assisted in learning traditional skills by using the first language of the learner along with English. It provided procedures for such language accommodation for learners needing such assistance. It also provided for instructional services in English as a second language.

The Equal Pay Act, 1963

In the United States, it was not uncommon for agencies, public and private, to discriminate on the basis of gender or race for the same work being done. Male teachers in some states were paid more than female teachers because they were deemed more valuable than females. In other places, African American teachers were paid less than Caucasian teachers because they were considered less valuable. Such practices were outlawed by the Equal Pay Act of 1963, even though some agencies had already discontinued the practice a few years earlier.

The Education Amendments, 1972
(Embracing Title IX on Gender Equity)

This legislation embraced Title IX on gender equity and included the provisions for equal access by females and males to athletic facilities and programming. This constituted a major change in American athletic programs as well as other activities because historically many sports had been limited to male participation. The equal distribution of rewards (scholarships, etc.) are also impacted by this legislation. Such changes are still being institutionalized in many programs as we near the Year 2000.

The Education for All Handicapped Act, 1975

This was a very comprehensive piece of legislation which provided for a more equitable educational program for exceptional learners in the United States through age twenty-one. It includes providing transportation for such persons to reach the school center as well as special training for teachers and others who would serve them. It was the ultimate in accommodation for such populations. Programmatically, it also helped non-exceptional persons understand this population much more directly, thus reducing the incidence of unconscious discrimination.

Today, one should add the Americans with Disabilities Act of 1991. All of this legislation impacted school districts in one way or another. Legal specialists have sought to avoid violations of provisions of these several acts. While the changes associated with such legal compliance have been underway for several years, there has been little attention to the provision of the content of the curriculum or the perspectives held by teachers regarding equity, diversity, and the academic socialization provided learners of all descriptions.

Why a Multicultural Transformation?

If the populations of schools are becoming more diverse, then the curriculum must also become more diverse. Again, however, we emphasize that if the population in a given school is not presently changing, then the program needs to change even more so that learners leave the school (at graduation or transfer) with the perspectives, competencies, and skills to function in a diverse society. Even though learners may not have had day-to-day experiences with culturally-different persons, their adult lives will likely bring them into contact with diversity through the workplace. Diversity carries a cultural richness which the curriculum, the teachers, and the students need. The skills needed in all walks of life today include a more sophisticated level of cross-cultural interaction. Diversity is becoming the rule for American institutions rather than the exception.

Equity is a concept which embraces fairness, justice, inclusiveness, balance, and a participation in schooling which prepares one for the American way of life. It is an intellectual concept which manifests itself in behavioral practices impacting humanity at large. A mentality of equity would suggest impartiality as a way of life, a mode of practice, and a framework from which all else emerges. Equity as a characteristic of the American mentality embracing curriculum would eliminate basic practices of discrimination (race discrimination, discrimination based on gender, age discrimination, economic discrimination, discrimination based on handicapping conditions and others) plus patterns of exclusion, dishonesty, partiality, and distorted perceptions.

The development of a mentality of equity through the curriculum requires some knowledge and commitment to the high principles on which America was founded. The commitment, however, must be deliberately expanded to include those Americans historically excluded from full participation in all that America has to offer. Such participation, however, will require some restructuring of many major institutions in our society so that cultural difference is respected, accommodated, and appreciated. Curriculum equity seeks to eliminate the social ills of racism, sexism, elitism, ageism, and ableism.

For Further Thought

1. Why do you think the United States is always so preoccupied with the scientific study of I.Q.? Are there social and political implications for studying intellect? Or intelligence?

2. How would you respond to professional (and non-professional) persons who still embrace the "melting pot" ideology for

curriculum and human services? What would you say to them? What is the reason that they should embrace diversity in the delivery of human services?

3. Why should researchers and educational practitioners avoid research activity that "blames the victim?" What is meant by blaming the victim?

4. Why, in your judgment, did we need national legislation (and state legislation) to dismantle practices which seemingly denied the reality of diversity in America?

5. What is equity?

6. Please prepare three points that you would make to those who deny that multiculturally transforming the curriculum is a necessary and desirable undertaking. In other words, how do you respond to the critics of such pluralistic upgrading?

7. "No one culture has a monopoly on knowledge!" (Baptiste). What does this mean to you? What implications are there for defining, developing, and evaluating curriculum?

References Cited

Banks, J.A. (1977). The implications of multicultural education for teacher education. In Klassen, F. & Gollnick, D. (eds.), *Pluralism and the American teacher: Issues and case studies*. Washington, DC: American Association of Colleges for Teacher Education, 1-30.

Coleman, J. (1966). *Equality of educational opportunity*. Washington, DC: Office of Education, U.S. Department of Health, Education and Welfare.

Cubberly, E. (1909). *Changing conceptions of education*. New York: Riverside Educational Mimeographs.

Della-Dora, D., *et. al*. (Eds.). (1974). *Education for an open society*. Washington, DC: Association for Supervision and Curriculum Development.

Fairchild, H.P. (1926). *The melting pot mistake*. Boston, MA: Little, Brown.

Ford, M. (1979). The development of an instrument for assessing levels of ethnicity in public school teachers. Unpublished doctoral dissertation,

University of Houston, Houston, TX.

Fuchs, L.H. (1990). *The American kaleidoscope: Race, ethnicity, and the civic culture*. Wesleyan, CT: The University Press of New England.

Gillie, O. (1977). Did Sir Cyril Burt fake his research on hereditability of intelligence? (Part 1). *Phi Delta Kappan*, February, 469-471.

Green, T.F. (1966). *Education and pluralism: Ideal and reality*. Twenty-sixth annual T. Richard Street Lecture, School of Education, Syracuse University, Syracuse, NY.

Jencks, C.S. *et al.* (1972). *Inequality: A reassessment of the effect of family and schooling in America*. New York: Basic Books.

Jensen, A.R. (1969). How much can we boost IQ and scholastic achievement? *Harvard Educational Review*, 39 (1), 1-123.

Kallen, H. (1956). *Cultural pluralism and the American idea*. Philadelphia, PA: University of Philadelphia Press.

Krug, M. (1976). *The melting of the ethnics*. Bloomington, IN: Phi Delta Kappa.

Labelle, T., & Ward, C. (1994). *Multiculturalism and education, diversity and its impact on schools and society*. Albany, NY: State University of New York Press.

Moynihan, D.P. (1965). *The Negro family: The case for national action*. Washington, DC: U.S. Department of Labor.

Myrdal, G. (1962). *An America dilemma: The Negro problem and modern democracy*. New York: Harper & Row.

Novak, M. (1973). *The rise of the unmeltable ethnics*. New York: Macmillan.

Pacheco, A. (1977). Cultural pluralism: A philosophical analysis. *Journal of Teacher Education*, May-June, 16-20.

Parsons, T. (1965). Full citizenship for the Negro American? in Parsons, T. & Clark, K.B. (Eds.), *The Negro American*. Boston, MA: Houghton-Mifflin.

Pratte, R. (1979). *Pluralism in education*. Springfield, IL: Charles C. Thomas.

Roosevelt, T. (1910). *Americanism*. [Speech given in 1910].

Sizemore, B. (1980). The politics of multicultural education. Unpublished manuscript.

Suzuki, B.H. (1979). Multicultural education: What's it all about? *Integrated Education*, 17 (1-2), 47-48.

Zangwill, I. (1922). *The melting pot: Drama in four acts*. New York: Macmillan. Originally produced in 1908.

Notes

No one culture
has a monopoly
on the development
of knowledge.

—H. Prentice Baptiste,
Jr.

Chapter 3

A Transformation
of the Curriculum

The Composition of the Curriculum

Years ago, a prevailing concept of the curriculum included the program of studies (English, mathematics, social studies, literature, music, art, drama, sciences, physical education, computer studies, and other subjects), the co-curriculum program of activities (those organized events and experiences like choral participation, athletic participation, band membership, photography clubs, cheerleading, student government participation, etc.) for which no grade is issued at the time of reporting to parents about progress, and the program of guidance which includes the standardized testing sequence and other counseling services. Because only the program of studies participation is permanently included on transcripts, it is often considered the most significant. Our position, along with others (Cortes, 1995, and Gay, 1995) is that such a structural procedure may have flaws in the age of diversity.

The educational practitioner must remember that the curriculum is a composite of signs, symbols, and ceremonies. The signs and symbols make major statements about what is valued, what is significant, and what is essential to the endorsed American way of life. The ceremonies give dignity, visibility, and reward to those elements which have been prioritized by the institution of the school.

Transforming the Curriculum in This Age

The Age of Consumerism

This means that the consumer (the student) is a major stakeholder in the value of the curriculum experience and that the student's profile, family, language, economic status, and preferences must be considered in curriculum planning. If the consumer is different from the 1636 Boston Latin Grammar School student, then the curriculum must be different.

The Age of Information

This means that in our information society, the kind of information, the nature of information, and the quantity of information assumes roles more powerful than ever before. It is the curriculum practitioner—the teacher, the librarian, the counselor, the curriculum specialist, and the adminstrators—who makes major decisions about which information is of most worth. In the age of information, new information is critical to the process of the transformation. Also, the information being made available today is more diverse and comes to the consumer in more diverse ways. In the age of information, the educational practitioner must prioritize which information will be utilized because of time limitations in direct instruction.

The Age of Self-Definition

This means that the diversity of profiles will demand that we learn how people choose to be defined. This personal definition will also include the labels by which people prefer to be called. Additionally, it includes how people choose to be referred to in other categories. For example, whether one wishes to be called handicapped, exceptional, disabled, or a person with a handicapping condition or with an exceptionality. Each group will define itself and, in the age of diversity, those definitions will constantly change. One must be alert to the changes and must respond positively as a professional educator.

The Age of Options and Alternatives

This means that the channels through which teaching and learning occur will take many forms and several designs. Historically, any learner who could not or would not tolerate sitting quietly and "listening" to the teacher was considered an academic misfit. Subsequently, we placed them in alternative learning settings and called them "retarded" in some way because of their unwillingness to adjust to a "mass production" system of education. Today, we are in the age of alternative delivery systems, which includes the use of the computer, telephone, television, the information super highway, fax machines, and scores of other channels through which one can learn. It has been suggested that each classroom should have a telephone and a computer on every desk.

The Age of Authentic Voices

This means that curriculum workers must now include members of the group being studied in the design, implementation, and evaluation of the curriculum experiences about that group. In other words, if one is preparing a unit of work on African Americans as a people, then the literature used for such work must include information written by or created by African Americans. Only African Americans can really speak for African Americans. If a Native American or a member of another ethnic group attempts to create such information about African Americans, his or her voice will be a basic voice, not an authentic voice. The same would be true if an African American was developing curriculum materials about Native Americans.

The authentic voice brings a lifetime of experience as a member of that specific ethnic or cultural group to the information being disseminated. If the curriculum is a composite of signs, symbols, and ceremonies, then images offered through new information will be extremely powerful. No teacher, librarian, or curriculum specialist should ignore the profile of the authors or creators of materials to be employed.

The Age of Psychological Accommodation

The concept of psychological accommodation embraces the notion of nonverbal indexes, physical declarations, verbal interactions, behavioral clues, and similar factors which communicate acceptance and a state of preferred (desirable) inclusion. This further connotes a mental or psychological connectedness between the profile of the client-participant (the student) and the nature of the services being provided for that participant's experience.

In some way, that connectedness permits the client-participant to feel that the process of service provision is committed to that person's well-being, improvement, advancement, and long-term development. It is the antithesis of toleration and it is characteristic of the environment in which that service is provided. Further it embraces "service delivery patterns" in institutions which clients observe and assess in regard to client perception of levels of satisfaction. In American education, the psychological accommodation of culturally different learners (and in many instances, female clients) has left much to be desired. These voices today are among the strongest in calling for transformation.

Related Factors

1. Psychological accommodation emerges from the professional's definition of human service delivery. Are the professional's services committed to all human beings who come for services?

2. Psychological accommodation is dependent on the institution's (school's) concept of its image—and how significant that image is to all segments of our society.

3. Psychological accommodation emerges from the philosophy which one holds of institutional service in the age of diversity.

4. Psychological accommodation is dependent on one's understanding of client perception of service—and the value of that perception to professional human service deliverers. (All educators are human service deliverers).

For Further Thought

1. Is the curriculum limited to **subjects** taken in school?

2. What is meant by the "Age of Self-Definition?" Is this a legitimate descriptor of the academic and social times in which we live?

3. What is meant by the "Age of Authentic Voice?" Why is this a necessary consideration in the delivery of human services?

4. What is meant by the "Age of Psychological Accommodation?" What would be some indicators of psychological accommodation?

5. What are the theoretical implications of the excerpt on page 46 (Boyer) for school curricula? What could be some interpretations of this excerpt?

References Cited

Cortes, C. (1995). Mass media as multicultural curriculum: Public competitor to school education. *Multicultural Education*, 2 (3), Spring, 4-7.

Gay, G. (1995). Curriculum theory and multicultural education. In Banks, J. & Banks, C. (Eds.), *Handbook of research on multicultural education*. New York: MacMillan Publishing Co., 25-43.

Character has no color.
Integrity has no age.
Honesty has no gender.
Compassion has no
height or weight.
Caring has no language.
Connecting has no handicap.
Relationships have no
degrees or certificates.

—James B. Boyer

Chapter 4

Boyer's Stages
of Ethnic Growth

Fragile Work Relations
and Curriculum Transformation

While America is managing the "information explosion" and the impact of technology, we seem to have failed in all aspects of human relationships—especially those relationships with people who differ from ourselves in one way or another. This has impacted the workplace to the extent that employers are now calling for new levels of competency so that entry-level workers are able to function with colleagues and supervisors who are culturally different from themselves.

The curriculum has a responsibility to address such workplace relations, since today's learners must ultimately work in diverse employment settings. Historically, such relations were considered a low priority within curriculum matters. The transformation of the curriculum is expected to result in such skills receiving much higher priority. Poor workplace relations are among the most costly in today's world, both in terms of productivity and the low quality of life too frequently experienced in the workplace.

Objectives of a Multicultural Transformation
(Re: Curriculum)

An overriding objective of the school curriculum is the accompaniment of a "social justice agenda." We are—or educators are—still dismantling a caste-system mentality which has crippled this country for centuries. The school curriculum which touches the life of every learner must assume a major responsibility for a social justice agenda. No one should ever be penalized for realities over which they had or have no control. Such realities include one's first language, race, gender, ethnic identity, economic state, or disabling condition. Because the school curriculum is a pervasive, "programmed experience" which everyone pursues, America can only reach its goal of equity through such curricular exposure.

Another objective of the transformation is the destruction of stereotypes. A stereotype is a standard mental picture held in common by many members of one group about another which represents an oversimplified opinion, affective attitude, or uncritical judgment. It is a preconceived or pre-judged idea about a group of people, even though all such groups have diverse membership. While there are positive stereotypes, the most frequent reference is to those reflecting undesirable characteristics. While this concept often has racial, ethnic, or economic connotations, stereotypes often refer to other characteristics as well. When distorted concepts are held, then behaviors and services are proportionately distorted for populations in question.

Increasing Ethnic Literacy

Another objective of the multicultural transformation of the curriculum is an increase in ethnic literacy for all Americans as they experience the school curriculum. Because of the traditional monocultural characteristics of the curriculum, the level of ethnic literacy of America's graduates has been extremely low. However, the recent increase in multiethnicity of school populations means that educators must embrace the implementation of an ethnically diverse curriculum. Coming generations need a new perspective on what really constitutes America: its people. Ethnic literacy refers to the cognitive information and sociological framework within which various ethnic/racial groups function in America.

Ethnically diverse populations will be requesting that those providing instructional services hold a much higher level of ethnic literacy about their identities than has previously been held. For example, many teachers have difficulty with the following test:

1. Name two African American playwrights.
2. Name two Mexican American historians.
3. Name two Native American writers or poets.
4. Name two Puerto Rican actors or actresses.
5. Name two female inventors or scientists.

Many presumably well-educated Americans who work with the curriculum find themselves unable to answer those questions, yet hold credentials which authorize them to provide instructional services to African American students, Mexican American students, Native American students, Puerto Rican students, Asian American students, as well as both male and female learners.

The difficulty with a diverse knowledge base about people has been the result of a commitment to the "classic studies in Arts and Sciences" which limited everyone to the study of people with the following profile:

1. Of European descent;
2. Caucasian;

3. Middle income or higher economic status;
4. English speaking (as a first language);
5. Male gender.

Our position is that while this profile represents strong contributions to the American way of life, it is much too limiting to adequately define an American. Increased diversity is now the basis for a transformed curriculum. Formerly a classic education categorically excluded studies about culturally different populations in our society. The transformation will deliberately embrace such profiles.

Boyer's Eight Stages of Ethnic Growth

The academic self-concept of all learners will dictate the level of involvement and achievement experienced with any schooling endeavor. As one grows as an organism, one experiences several levels of growth and development. Those whose research focuses on child growth and development have, until recently, ignored the cultural, racial, social, and related factors associated with human development. All socialization emerges from the totality of one's experiences and those experiences take place in an environment communicating many messages. Such messages are central to the value placed on one's ethnic identity. In other words, one looks for reflections of one's family, race, language, religion, music, recreative practices, and art. Further, such expectations, when not met, deliver a powerful message of rejection, illegitimacy, and questionable academic involvement to the learner.

A psycho-social instructional connectedness occurs within learners when they subconsciously identify with, or relate to, the human profile or human event which constitutes the required content for study in school. This includes the (1) nature of the story, (2) the conclusions drawn from direct story-telling, and (3) the indirect messages delivered as a result of story lines. It goes without saying that the element of academic evaluation and the total curricular ecology are impacted by the nature of this environmental reality.

One grows in a variety of ways both as a learner and as an individual. An adult worker grows in the workplace. One grows in one's career. In all of these areas, that growth is directly tied to one's human profile. In all stages of growth and development, one learns valuable lessons as well as what to value and what to discard based on instructional emphasis. The growth being described here is the combination of psycho-social realization growth that one's personhood, one's life, one's expected activities, and one's race, language, customs, family, and behavior are all seen by others from some frame of reference. That frame of reference is largely defined by the totality of the academic environment, and by directed learning experiences. All required experiences in the schooling process can serve to enhance that apprehension or to decrease it.

Ethnic Growth and Academic Achievement

Because of the strong connection between ethnic growth and academic achievement, the selection and use of curriculum materials reflecting diversity are critical dimensions of the schooling process. The following stages of ethnic growth are identified for describing a series of experiences by learners. They are intentionally listed in reverse order (highest to lowest) to emphasize the significance of the stages:

> Stage 8 - Celebration
> Stage 7 - Appreciation
> Stage 6 - Respect
> Stage 5 - Acceptance
> Stage 4 - Recognition

Stage 3 - Tolerance
Stage 2 - Existence
Stage 1 - Non-Existence

Our position is that the higher the stage of ethnic growth, the greater the potential for academic achievement. Any higher stage of ethnic growth, however, cannot be maintained without constant nurturing and exposure. The lowest stages of ethnic growth could result in self-hatred, self-rejection, and ethnic self-denial due to the consistent messages of exclusion and non-endorsement received by one experiencing curricular interaction (Banks, 1977).

Each stage is described in the following section. They are intended to identify what a learner experiences when interacting with the daily curriculum of the school. There is considerable evidence to suggest that role models, images, profiles, and connectedness are powerful elements of one's ethnic identity and growth. While ethnic growth can occur in adulthood, researchers suggest that the major psychological thrust of early childhood in life is the development and mastery of self as an independent human being, which comes with a willingness to extend experiences beyond the family.

The Stages

Stage 1: Non-Existence

This is a psycho-social stage of development regarding the ethnic value of one's profile. It is considered the lowest level of growth (or retardation) because it is essentially the absence of any cultural, racial, or linguistic elements (including family profiles) in the content and process of schooling interaction. This absence communicates that certain client profiles do not legitimately exist and are not endorsed by the school. For example, if a Native American first grade learner begins the schooling experience attempting to learn to read, he or she begins to look for families like his or her family. To be able to see people like one's self represents a confirmation of legitimate existence.

Such absence precludes a constant reminder of humanity which reflects one's profile as part of the daily on-going curriculum experience. It essentially forces one to study profile after profile without experiencing any psychological comfort regarding that content. The learner internalizes what is acceptable and what is not acceptable based on what has been included or excluded from the daily content in the early stages of reading and learning.

A strong message received by the new learner is that his or her kind of category of humanity does not warrant endorsement by the major institution of the American school. (Remember that the school is the only major institution in our society in which there is a legal requirement for the child's involvement and/or interaction). To the learner, the ultimate message of this stage is:

"I don't exist in this institution."
"People like me are not appreciated in this experience."
"Apparently, people like me are not significant in the
  schooling process."
"Nothing in this story reflects my family."

Subsequently, the question arises for the learner: "Why should I pursue these tasks in an environment which fails to include people like me—profiles like mine?"

Stage 2: Existence

In this stage of ethnic growth, the learner is aware that there are now some minimal indications that persons like one's self do exist. As reflected in curriculum materials and instructional delivery, there is still little or no interactive value, but at least there is inclusion as opposed to total absence from what must be studied in school.

This stage permits the learner to assume that his/her profile is at least a segment of American humanity. It is not a powerful segment, because the "interactive" level is so low. It is, at best, a member of the audience rather than a significant actor in the theater of life.

Existence, however, is a much more enhancing stage than non-existence. Existence—as compared to absence—makes its own statement and silently announces potential for a more functional level of inclusion—but little else. The message for the learner, though, is "at least I'm included."

It is to be understood that these stages of ethnic growth are not always clearly understood by the learner/client because one's period of socialization in any phase of life is rarely or clearly understood. It is often frustrating and confusing. Because stages of ethnic growth are so aligned with the value which one places on one's self, it is critically important that educators understand the significance attached to content by learners of all descriptions.

When a learner's stage of ethnic growth is at this level, it might seem almost impossible to experience success in the school endeavor. Psychological implications of learning tell us that one needs to see one's self in the curriculum in order to do well—to achieve—with that curriculum. Such a limited level of inclusion guarantees limited success (and/or participation) with traditional achievement indexes for those impacted directly by such limitation.

Stage 3: Tolerance

Several years ago, well-meaning groups and agencies promoted the concept of tolerance (racial tolerance, linguistic tolerance, etc.). While these concepts may have been appropriate for the times, today's populations do not find toleration an adequate response to human diversity. The concept of tolerance embraces "the capacity of an organism to grow or thrive when subjected to unfavorable environmental factors." Knowledgeable researchers, social scientists, and educators agreed that some elements of an unfavorable environment existed for many learners and toleration seemed to be an appropriate goal.

Toleration also implies the existence of some entity which is not officially sanctioned, not readily deemed an on-going part of the endorsed setting or format. Toleration also suggests that "something is an allowable deviation from standard services or expectations."

The human entity (especially the culturally different) understood that racial tolerance (and all its antecedents) were less than the factors freely enhancing growth of people. Academic growth is critically related to the ecological factors of schooling, including the personal views taken of learners by professional educators.

There are several curricular manifestations at the tolerance level. When learners experience the toleration level of inclusion within curriculum matter, one quickly discovers the limiting forces of rejection through endorsement. The human species associates toleration with suffering for both those tolerating and those being tolerated. This environmental arrangement seems inappropriate for both parties.

Classroom inclusion of curriculum materials reflecting learners at such limiting levels delivers strong messages to culturally different children about the validity of their existence and to other children that America is primarily a country in which selected groups, races, and people are officially endorsed. The school's message, delivered primarily through the curriculum, announces the level of human growth to be experienced by learners. One of the most powerful instruments for delivery of such messages is the content, form, style, and emphasis of curriculum materials.

When curricular experiences and the utilization of minimally diverse curriculum materials comprise the standard level of ecological involvement for learners, then ethnic growth is thereby restricted.

Stage 4: Recognition

This stage of ethnic growth is placed slightly higher than the stage of toleration. Recognition implies:

   a. Acknowledging or taking notice of;
   b. Formal acknowledgement;
   c. To admit as being of some particular status;
   d. The sensing of special notice.

Stage 5: Acceptance

This stage is the first full stage during which the learner gets a message of "inclusion without pretext." It embraces the following:

   a. To be regarded as proper, normal, or inevitable;
   b. To be received into the mind with some degree of attachment to truth;
   c. To be received favorably within the context of curricular entity;
   d. To be viewed as part of an entity from the perspective of being willingly inducted into such whole;
   e. To experience some degree of favorable response to the existence of such presence in the on-going curricular interaction.

Messages delivered to learners through curricular experience (but particularly through curriculum materials) at the level of acceptance are essentially messages of consent. They communicate the positive notions of "institutionalization of diversity" within the context of public and private education. In addition to the "message of consent," learners experience some degree of legality with diverse presence. In other words, America now views such presence as normal for instructive interaction, but goes beyond to embrace views of strengths, assets, and contributions.

While acceptance is normally perceived as the "other side" of rejection, this academic emotion goes beyond that stage. Rejection implies refusal, rebuttal, repellent. In this context, acceptance surpasses the alternate stage of rejection because it includes the expanded concept of "being designed for favorable inclusion." In our eight-stage scenario, this stage is clearly the beginning of the top half of the academic emotions experienced by learners.

The acceptance stage also reflects strong instructional style factors which communicate degrees of value and worth to entities and human presence. The instructional style embraces a mode of expressing thought in language growth being experienced by learners. In other words, what teachers think of such inclusion tends to be immediately communicated to learners. The significance of instructional thought is critical to the development of self-concept in learners. In a society which has a history of religion, learners experience various stages of growth evolving from day-to-day nonverbal messages of classroom involvement.

The instructional style also reflects the manner or tone assumed in learner interaction.

Stage 6: Respect

This stage of ethnic growth involves the psycho-social feeling of being viewed by others as having significant worth within any given environment. This stage suggests that one's ethnic/cultural profile is acknowledged as culturally distinct with unique characteristics worthy of emulation.

The patterns of life and the adopted values are felt to be esteemed and highly regarded. Synonyms of this concept include honor, admiration, reverence, consideration, courtesy, positive attention, homage, and significance.

When the learner reaches this stage of ethnic growth, he or she experiences a sense of value among different entities. The sense of being adequate, being equal to other entities, and being perceived by others as being of endorsed value are all continuing dimensions of learner psychological accommodation.

The learner's ethnic profile is utilized by the curriculum program (through teacher selection of materials including that profile) to the extent that other learners adopt such endorsement as worthy of emulation. The nature of such inclusion also represents a highly positive, productive view of that person's ethnic profile—often also including the gender profile. Such approval of the existence of one profile moves the psycho-social level to one of consent and approval by being "held up" as one of several models of human existence.

To be respected often implies that positive impressions have been made in numerous circumstances. This stage of ethnic growth precedes the higher level of celebration in which the level of psychological accommodation provides the essential freedom for one to participate in the celebration of one's own profile/ ethnicity.

This stage also implies an element of deserving recognition. It represents the other end of "disgraceful or disreputable" as an image to be perpetuated.

Respect may generate a sense of "admirable intimidation," but never reflects elements of fear. It continues to provide an avenue through which ethnicity may be developed and positive self-concept emerges as a result of environmental messages delivered to learners.

Stage 7: Appreciation

This stage involves the positive essentiality of accommodation through on-going image inclusion. The positive visualization of one's profile sends curricular/psychological messages of adequacy as a human being to those involved with such materials/images. These contribute to the conceptualization and reinforcement of self-concept—and whether a learner is a child or an adult, he or she experiences much of the same infusion of positive essentiality. This positive essentiality embraces those elements which communicate the legitimacy of existence plus the acceptability of one's profile as a legitimate curricular element. Remembering that what the school endorses becomes legitimate cultural content, one seeks to have pluralistic profiles incorporated at the level of appreciation rather than at lower levels.

Many curricular specialists concerned with stages of ethnic growth as reflected through exposure to curriculum materials often adopt tolerance and/or appreciation as the only stages of instructional design. Because this discussion is initiated from the learner's perspective, the additional stages (7 and 8) are employed because of the deliberate but progressive growth stages through which the human organism travels.

Academic growth is always somewhat imprecise, depending on the instruments employed to assess such growth. Indeed, much of curriculum is imprecise, but the long-range impact of ethnic growth (emerging, in part, from the day-to-day uses of curriculum materials) cannot be overestimated.

In this context, the curriculum worker responsible for choosing curriculum materials should embrace an understanding of the levels on which such content is included and/or presented. In other words, what are the messages delivered to learners as a result of using these materials with this learner-population? To what extent does the learner feel appreciated as a human entity? Does the use of these materials (reflecting the images/roles included) communicate positive essentials to the learners being asked to absorb them?

Stage 8: Celebration

Beyond all other levels of ethnic growth experienced by the individual is the level of celebration. By definition, celebration means to commemorate, to observe joyfully, to observe with formal rites, to honor, to praise, to install, to salute, to illuminate, to signalize, to inaugurate, to rejoice, to toast, to make merry.

Each of these synonyms helps to define part of the individual stages of evolvement experienced by the learner when his or her ethnic profile is so institutionalized that a feeling of celebration emerges. The internalized celebration which denotes a higher level of legitimacy than all others also permits jubilation and/or coronation of one's ethnicity. To the learner whose ethnic/racial profile has historically signaled defeat, exclusion, negative stereotypes, negative reinforcement elements, the celebration level represents triumph, victory, and fanfare.

It is difficult to describe the transformation from exclusion (non-existence) all the way up to celebration for learners whose total school experience (as positively reflected through curriculum materials) has been a series of questionable conclusions. Absence from the large number of textbooks, supplementary materials, and other school-endorsed data can cause major feelings of negativism in one's academic self-concept.

When one reaches the stage of celebration, he or she experiences a significant, unifying, culturally-induced, qualitative emotion considered psychologically healthy to the point of enhancing mental health and academic security.

It signals a festive freedom for active participation in the larger society at a level devoid of apprehension, devoid of negative environmental responses which inhibit sharing. It embraces visual literacy and ethnic literacy which can be used to influence the perspective of others who might share in the experience of celebration.

The increasing development of ethnic museums and galleries represents the growing awareness of the role which these institutions play is enhancing the celebration stage of ethnic growth. Museums offer a healthy memory which provides more protection from the erosion of time for positive events and they retain memories of pain and pleasure and help individuals and society to call up interpretations of past events when they are needed. The stage of ethnic celebration permits an endorsement of these interpretations by all persons, but it is especially significant to the ethnic/racial groups whose history, sociology, music, literature, dance, art, and recreation have been systematically excluded from the endorsed program—the curriculum—of the American school.

During this stage, the individual often becomes an advocate for increased employment of such materials in order to actualize the possibilities for those learners (children and adults) whose academic self-concept may be under-developed. Learning in the museum, however, is largely visual, while classroom learning emphasizes books and words (interaction) as ways of learning.

Where Does One Begin the Transformation?
(Re: Multicultural Transformation)

All curriculum development begins in the minds of people. Curriculum programming is based on the philosophical foundations of those who are responsible for shaping the learning experiences of any given group. The leadership of curriculum effort must understand that multicultural education is an area about which very few people are "philosophically neutral" because it is an area of curriculum reform which provides a "friendly confrontation" with the tradition of the curriculum, a movement towards inclusiveness.

People across the country who are highly visible in printed literature, in the electronic media, and in our communities have voiced their opposition to the transformation of the school's curriculum toward a more accurate portrayal of all Americans—both those enrolled and those not in one's given geographic area.

The first activity is to help curriculum workers understand the need for upgrading the curriculum toward these levels of equity and inclusiveness. We must help them to understand that the curriculum is the lifeblood of the American school system and that it serves to transform our young people into literate, functioning adults. It is with this in mind that the leadership must use cognitive data, logical attestations, and professional influence to help others embrace this upgrading.

It should be remembered that most adults today were academically socialized with a monocultural curriculum and thus many struggle with the assumption that their own education was either inappropriate or inadequate—especially if they are educational professionals (people who teach in and administer the schools).

Further, the ethnic socialization of many professionals was devoid of childhood experiences (prior to age eighteen) which brought them academically or socially in contact with cultural difference—at least as an equal entity. There must be efforts to help professional educators accept the tenets of multicultural curriculum even though their own public education did not embrace such levels of diversity. Those charged with leadership of public schools must use all their creative energies to assist those for whom these ideas are new. Leadership of curriculum programs involving the transformation to a multicultural level will require the best that is known about persuasive leadership that will move forward without alienating those who are being influenced.

Because multicultural education involves more than mere intellectual awareness, strong leadership is essential in helping professionals (and sometimes parents) understand its role, scope, and function. One suggestion would be to include persons expressing the greatest opposition to development in the planning stages of curriculum improvement. From these experiences, many have become advocates for multicultural upgrading of school programs.

For Further Thought

1. What are some of the objectives of a multicultural transformation? How should we respond to those who do not see such objectives as a high priority for the curriculum or for human service delivery?

2. What is a policy? What is a curriculum policy? How does a policy differ from a procedure?

3. Is it still necessary to reduce stereotypes? Why? Why not?

4. One of the stages of ethnic growth is tolerance. Is this a necessary stage? Is there a difference between tolerance and toleration? Is this level more associated with the human condition (or human relations) than some others? Discuss your response.

5. Celebration is another stage of ethnic growth. Some persons have great difficulty with the notion of "cultural or ethnic celebration" as a stage or concept. Including it as the highest stage of ethnic growth is not psychologically palatable to many. Please assume that you are part of a panel whose objective is to convince or persuade the critics of this stage. Outline the six major points you would make before your audience. Explain or justify each point.

References Cited

Banks, J.A. (1977). The implications of multicultural education for teacher education. In Klassen, F. & Gollnick, D. (Eds.), *Pluralism and the American teacher*. Washington, DC: American Association of Colleges for Teacher Education, 1-30.

Boyer, J.B. (1990). *Curriculum materials for ethnic diversity*. Lawrence, KS: Center for Black Leadership and Development, University of Kansas.

Other References

Athanases, S.Z., Christiano, D., & Lay, E. (1995). Fostering empathy and finding common ground in multiethnic classes. *English Journal*, 84 (9), 26.

Bachman, J. (1994). Multicultural education: A program to benefit our students and society. *NASSP Bulletin*, 78 (11), 68.

Carpenter, K.D. (1994). Achieving a true multicultural focus in today's curriculum. *NASSP Bulletin*, 78 (6), 62.

Kreidler, W.J. (1995). Say good-bye to bias. *Instructor*, 104 (1), 28.

Nixon, H.L. & Henry, W.J. (1992). White students at the black university: Their experiences regarding acts of racial intolerance. *Equity and Excellence*, 25 (3), 121.

Peters, W. (1987). *A class divided then and now*. New Haven, CT: Yale Univeristy Press.

Whiting, A.N. (1991). *Guardians of the flame: Historically black colleges yesterday, today, and tomorrow*. Washington, DC: American Association of State Colleges and Universities.

Unity is the
foundation
of a diverse society.
Diversity is the
foundation of an
equitable curriculum.

—James B. Boyer

Chapter 5

Institutionalizing a Multicultural Curriculum

Institutionalizing Multicultural Education

In many curriculum efforts, the process involves the following:

Theory ——> Practice ——> Institutionalization

Institutionalization involves helping a reform effort to become accepted by those participating in the school (curriculum institution). *It is important to remember that the theory of multicultural inclusiveness involves helping people embrace diversity as a way of life.* This will require patience, skill, and academic tenacity.

Multiculturalizing Subject Areas of the Curriculum

Efforts to transform the American school curriculum from a

monocultural entity to a multicultural experience will require serious analysis of all school learnings and the instruction through which such learnings occur. This chapter includes a compilation of ideas which could be used as beginning efforts to make the transformation by professional educators engaged in such endeavors.

Several subject-matter areas have been specified for content and/or instructional considerations. The following assumptions are identified for any person or persons attempting to implement the ideas included here:

1. That educators will attempt to preserve the dignity of all learners who come for academic services.

2. That serious efforts will be undertaken to provide culturally-responsive instruction to all learners.

3. That the conceptualization of the Multicultural Transformation will be seen as America's effort to have its major institutions become more aligned with the major documents of our society—particularly the *Constitution of the United States*, the *Bill of Rights*, and the *Declaration of Independence*.

4. That appropriate staff development will be undertaken to assist educators in developing the competencies for instructional delivery required to reach this level of academic development.

It is our hope that the ideas here will be useful to serious educators in attempting to transform the American school curriculum both for culturally different rural and urban learners and for European Caucasian learners who must live in a more diverse world than ever imagined in the history of this country.

English and Language Arts Curriculum

1. Include poems by culturally-different poets—especially those representing African American, Hispanic American, Asian American and Native American backgrounds.

2. Examine anthologies to be sure they reflect both basic and authentic authors.

3. Female authors from several different cultural-ethnic groups should be included among items students are required to read.

4. Poets like Langston Hughes, Joy Harjo, Gwendolyn Brooks, and others should be part of the language arts program.

5. Ask students to bring one piece of literature to class which they would like to read, interpret, and discuss.

6. Have students write essays on what it would be like to be of a different ethnic or racial identity than they are. What would be the advantages or other realities of such difference?

7. Provide students with biographies, autobiographies, and magazines which depict language arts elements dealing with African Americans, Hispanic Americans, Asian Americans, and Native Americans.

8. Incorporate diverse content through the substance of storylines, and in all forms of composition.

9. Begin to think of author-identification of short stories, poetry, books, and other literary elements.

10. Utilize ethnically identifiable newspapers, magazines, brochures, etc.

11. Interpret the substance of speech patterns and communicative styles which bear identifiable cultural or even geographic distinctions.

12. Have students interview persons (human resources) of non-European background (both in and out of the community).

13. Examine stereotypes which may be found in the substance of television, in drama—including community theatre, film, published articles, etc.

14. Conduct a continuous critical analysis of children's litera-

ture for images of diverse populations—and possible implications.

15. Help students recognize that one language is not better than another.

16. Counter ethnocentrism in all aspects of poetry and other literary documentation.

17. Literary anthologies should include works by Black authors, Hispanic authors, Native American authors, Asian American authors, and female authors.

18. Use folklore to discover cultural orientation.

19. Consistently explore multiple perspectives on the same event, idea, or practice. Seek to include both the historical significance and the sociological significance—as seen by various cultural groups.

20. Examine subject area titles for overt or covert messages of ethnocentrism or/and oppression. Titles such as English Literature, American Literature, and The Classics must be examined for their subtle oppressive messages.

Social Studies Curriculum

1. Include the study of the history of Asian Americans (a large diverse group), African Americans, Native Americans, Mexican Americans and other Hispanic groups, as well as Native Americans. The history of European Americans will always be part of the American school curriculum and it is reinforced through the mass media on a daily basis.

2. Explore concepts of exploitation, oppression, discrimination, and bias as reflected in current data. Do not hesitate to use census data, current demographic trends, and economic data to analyze these concepts—and always with particular attention to the impact on culturally different people and women.

3. Have students view films or other visuals in which culturally-different people are in leadership roles and non-traditional roles.

4. Compare median incomes of culturally-different groups with others and build discussions around why these data look as they do and especially what all people can do to change such realities.

5. Compare median incomes of males to females in the workplace. Discuss why these figures look as they do and what both males and females can do to change inequitable outcomes.

6. Study the history of your state (or of America) with particular attention to the perceptions and concerns of ethnic/racial minorities and of women.

7. Expand the study of African Americans beyond a unit on slavery to include contributions by African Americans and political analyses of the subject.

8. Expand the study of Hispanic Americans beyond wars and similar events to include the political perspectives of these groups, both now and in the past.

9. Analyze group preferences and concerns (including the social realities and views) of groups like Native Americans, Puerto Ricans, etc.

10. Social studies programs should definitely include knowledge about Native American tribes represented in your state and region.

11. There should be definite attempts to sociologically review the concepts of family, groups, community, etc.

12. Review perspectives on Chicano history, Native American history, Puerto Rican history, Japanese history, and other relevant groups.

13. Employ the "minority report" approach.

14. Role play town meetings on the rights of women to vote.

15. Role play town meetings on the rights of African Americans, Native Americans, Asian Americans, and Hispanic Americans to serve as city commissioners, mayors, and governor of your state.

16. In geography-related classes, have students research different African countries.

17. Traditional linear approaches and organizational patterns (time and direction) for history should be considered highly inappropriate because they often present various cultural/ethnic groups in superior/inferior inequitable settings.

NOTE: Social studies learnings should always assume that the disciplines of social science seek to positively influence the quality of life for all people.

Elementary Education Curriculum

1. Almost all areas of the elementary curriculum lend themselves to exploration into culturally-different content and perspectives. The creativity of the teacher will determine the extent to which such elements are operationalized.

2. Elementary curriculum activity is an excellent place to enhance ethnic literacy, and this can be done through calendars, holidays (those considered significant by Mexican Americans, African Americans, Jewish Americans, Native Americans, Puerto Rican Americans, Asian Americans, and others), and events of celebration comprehended by young children. Instructional recognition should be given to such holidays and events—particularly those which are commonly associated with culturally-different groups.

3. Attention should also be given to women's contributions to the American way of life. Contributions to invention, science, technology, and politics are critically important in these times of curriculum and societal transformation, and units on women's contributions are especially significant and needed.

4. Elementary science programs which address scientific literacy from the consumer's point of view should be emphasized, particularly on issues involving toxic waste, water-related services, etc.

5. Elementary social studies programs should seek to really pluralize geography, community, ethnic studies, and economic studies as key parts of the emphasis on transformation.

6. Elementary social studies programs should seek to reflect Africa, Asia, Mexico, and South America as well as Europe.

7. Elementary reading programs should acknowledge the power of indirect learning. Illustrations, photographs, and other visual elements included in materials being used in the teaching of reading are vitally important in delivering messages of equity.

8. Children's literature must acknowledge and endorse Native American culture, African American culture, Hispanic perspectives, and Asian folklore.

9. Elementary language arts programs should explore how fiction and other literary works by American ethnic authors share cultural components of culturally-diverse groups.

10. Elementary mathematics programs should explore the relationships between the number system used within a given society and what that society holds as culturally or ethnically significant. Elementary mathematics programs ought to emphasize contributions made to our number system by culturally-different groups.

11. Elementary instruction should nurture the oral tradition of African American learners by bringing it to the classroom. Special attention should be given to the role of the African American church in the familial socialization of children. This is also significant for Hispanic families and their traditional association with the institution of the church.

12. Elementary instruction should address and confront theories of racial inferiority and racial superiority.

13. Elementary instruction should embrace a responsibility for promoting concepts of nonviolence on an ongoing basis. Some people consider academic violence, including curriculum bias, to be as serious as physical violence.

14. Elementary instruction should explore the concept of testing and all of its perceptions, ramifications, and emphases. It may be necessary to deliberately teach test-taking skills in order to reduce the inequities in testing now perceived by most culturally different communities.

15. Elementary instruction should never underestimate the impact of poverty on learners, on learning styles, and on instruction.

Science and Health Curriculum

Because the fields of science, health, and environmental studies are so closely tied to present-day concepts of human preservation, the multicultural transformation of these fields is now essential. Earlier, the culturally-different populations now under study perceived these fields as something less than consumer-friendly to persons like themselves. Today, there are many persons who feel that these fields focused very heavily on specialists for the fields—in preference to a consumer benefit emphasis. Following are some considerations for multicultural transformation today:

1. Focus on consumer scientific literacy, especially among populations considered culturally-different. For those populations considered culturally the same, one must consider economic and exceptional factors which the scientific community appears to forget.

2. While the consumer focus is urgent and necessary, this does not mean that specialists in these fields should not be part of the focus of the future. New specialists, however, should reflect the diversity and demographic trends now in the American mosaic. African Americans, Hispanic Americans, Native Americans, Asian Americans, and women from all groups should be part of this new group of science specialists. (Some estimates are that such groups make up less than three percent of the active scientific specialists today).

3. Give deliberate attention to bio-ethics as an ongoing factor in the scientific community.

4. Check the science program for the inclusion of female inventors, health and medical specialists, and environmentalists.

5. Examine the science program for the inclusion of scientists like Ernest Just, Charles R. Drew, Barbara McClintock, Luis W. Alvarez, and Chien Shiung Wu.

6. Health-related science programs should give deliberate attention to the AIDS crisis, citing trends, causes, and responses. Additional attention should be given to the pediatric AIDS crisis. Also focus on responses to health-related problems in the various culturally-diverse communities.

7. Examine the role of agencies like the Food and Drug Administration.

8. Develop consciousness of the toxic waste index in any given area. How are decisions made about where toxic waste shall be placed?

9. Include the study of information on cancer research.

10. Include work on biologist Charles Turner and inventor Granville T. Woods.

11. New information indicates that we are having an upsurge in the incidences of infectious disease in America.

12. How are decisions made about who shall get organ donations?

13. Identify persons of note, such as famous chemists and others, whose contributions support our lifestyles today.

14. Scientific instruction should increase options for visual thinking while remembering the impact of indirect learning.

15. The scientific community must avoid the practice of attributing biological causes to social behavior.

16. Elimination of the traditionally elitist attitude of science instruction is a must.

Mathematics Curriculum

The field of mathematics has often limited its work to the specificity of non-human theories and computational practice. The transformation now being proposed includes deliberate attention to the human dimension of the numbering system, the computational framework, and the meaning behind all quantitative activity.

In the case of economically poor learners, the field of mathematics might do well to connect ancestorally to populations who have heretofore felt unwelcome to pursue fields whose image and reality involved mathematics. The following are suggestions:

1. Include the study of culturally different persons who made contributions to the field of mathematics in the regular mathematics program. Such activity serves to provide for ancestral connectedness for those students representing those ethnic profiles. For other students, it serves to announce contributions to mathematics by those who represent difference.

2. It would be good to identify persons of note in mathematics whose contributions support our lifestyles today.

3. Identify the origins of number systems, etc.

4. Explore the cultural orientation to the learning of mathematical concepts. How are such numerical concepts learned best by Native American learners? by African American learners?

5. Examine word problems to discover if stereotypical concepts are being included therein.

6. Examine word problems to discover if sexist language is used or if any accompanying illustrations imply the victimization of either males or females.

7. Do not hesitate to examine consumer practices which result in the exploitation of people based on color, ethnic group, or gender.

8. Do not limit the study of mathematics to various formulas without adding consumer concepts to such study. Also, be sure to include basic concepts of money management in multicultural mathematics instruction.

Human Ecology (Home Economics) Curriculum

Because of the dramatic changes in the structure, style, and functioning of the American family, this field has tremendous potential for participating in the transformation of the American school curriculum. It should be remembered that the research on child development, family studies, nutritional practices of Americans, preventive health concerns, and elements of studies on clothing and textiles carry major implications for curriculum activity which embraces cultural and ethnic diversity. The following are suggestions related thereto:

1. Emphasize a gender-balanced view of homemaking and home management, including child care.

2. Move from traditional basic nutritional lessons to an understanding of ethnic foods and their meaning.

3. Help students move from traditional (non-informed) purchasing practices to culturally-referenced consumer skills.

4. Transpose curricular offerings from "Bachelor Living" courses to alternatives and options for consumers. The idea is for more inclusive language.

5. Explore, study, and include diverse family profiles. Not all people live in families of two parents, etc. (Some forty percent of all elementary school children live in one-parent homes or similar settings).

6. The clothing-textile program should reflect styles and designs from Europe, but also from Asia, Africa, Mexico, and South America as well as other places. The intent is to move from "quaint" perceptions of difference to a genuine respect for the diversity in cultures represented in America.

7. What role does climate play in the ongoing development of clothing styles in different sections of the United States as well as in different countries?

8. Human ecology should never underestimate the impact of poverty.

Journalism and Mass Communications Curriculum

The impact of mass communications on the lives of all Americans is greater today than anytime in the history of this country. Both the print media and the electronic media serve to shape opinions, to influence policy, to inform people in our information society, and to communicate cultural and ethnic heritage at levels heretofore unknown. Among the several considerations which specialists in this field should give to multicultural transformation are the following:

1. All programs should utilize ethnic newspapers and ethnic magazines, both for skill training and for consumer concern considerations. The field of journalism is becoming more specialized every day. Magazine racks are loaded with such special market publications and students should be helped to understand the impact of this trend.

2. The electronic media is increasingly powerful. It has resulted in our living in a global village. Students should be helped to examine radio stations and other media whose marketing audience especially includes African Americans, Hispanic

Americans, and Asian Americans, along with Native Americans.

3. Teachers might especially assign students to watch documentaries and other programs on Public Television stations which address diversity and then write summaries and analyses of such efforts.

4. Students should be helped to understand the marketing of information, with due attention to race, language, ethnicity, exceptionality, and economics.

5. Finally, it is extremely important to teach learners how to detect journalism bias in all reporting and dissemination of information. News stories are powerful elements in shaping opinions and in preserving opportunities for all citizens. However, images are critically significant in these times.

Business and Technology Curriculum
(Comsumer Competence Via Business Education)

All learners will engage in consumer activities throughout their lives. This area of the curriculum is essential for a democracy and for the continued upgrading of the quality of life in America. Business education shares a unique place in the education of all learners, but especially in the lives of economically poor learners of all races, languages, cultures, and geographic regions.

In addition to broad occupational competence training which must embrace cross-cultural understandings in the workplace, this area must deliver services which emphasize greater consumer competence. Poverty is a major social problem in America (both rural and urban), and the following ideas or concepts are considered essential within this realm. This does not suggest an elimination of traditional skills of literacy, but rather an amplification of this area for a society growing more complex in its economic activities:

1. Understanding wholesale-retail-consumer relationships.
2. Skills in budgeting and planning (including cost analysis).

3. Installment buying (and costs associated therewith).

4. Understanding that an economic risk is the chance of loss of earning power or of property.

5. Understanding that economic risks are always present.

6. The concept of insurance—understanding that insurance is a plan for the distribution of loss.

7. Understanding that intelligence regarding money management requires the protection of property and income through insurance.

8. Understanding that an installment contract is a binding agreement and should be thoroughly understood before one enters into such an agreement.

9. Understanding that interest is the payment for the use of money and that there is a major difference in interest income and interest expense.

10. Understanding the necessity for making wise choices in the expenditure of one's money.

11. Understanding why banks customarily charge for rendering checking account services.

12. Understanding that the inconvenience and danger involved in carrying large sums of money on one's person may be avoided through the use of checking accounts or bank drafts.

13. Understanding that the major functions of businesses relate to the production of goods, to the distribution of goods, and to the satisfaction of the demand for different services.

Also, in the area of personal business skills:

14. Developing the skill of personal financial recordkeeping and safe storage of other important documents (birth certificates, school records, receipts, contracts, other legal documents, etc.).

15. Developing the skill of managing the family clothing, communications (telephone), and transportation budgets.

16. Understanding the impact of advertising and how consumer restraint must operate to control one's financial resources.

17. Understanding the operation of Social Security and other related programs impacting human consumer functioning.

18. Understanding taxes: sales tax, property tax, income tax, and the many other areas in which taxes impact our lives.

19. Government functioning and how it impacts our consumer lives, especially the management of our personal finances.

20. The regulatory role of many agencies, such as the Federal Communications Commission, the Federal Deposit Insurance Corporation, the Food and Drug Administration, etc.

21. Understanding the system for accommodating unemployed persons.

22. Understanding that with consumer rights come major consumer responsiblities.

Music Curriculum

The following ideas are offered by Horace Clarence Boyer of the Music Department at the University of Massachusetts:

1. Alternate the composers, periods, and styles over a two-year period, so that the symphony is replaced one year by the blues, opera is replaced at another time by Chicano folk songs, square dancing is replaced by Native American dances, etc. (Both elementary and secondary levels.)

2. In a comparative study of Afro-American Symphony and Negro Folk Symphony, try to select and identify those "characteristic" elements which are included. (Afro-American Symphony has as its first theme blues, and in the third movement employs a march reminiscent of the music which accompanied the "cake walk," while Negro Spirituals serve as the thematic material for Negro Folk Symphony). (Both elementary and secondary levels.)

3. Prepare a unit on the multiracial population of your city, county, or state, focusing on the music of each ethnic group. The research and preparation of the music might result in an assembly program for the entire school, or a presentation before another class. (Elementary level.)

4. Seek out a musical member of one or more ethnic groups

in your community who would be willing to come to your class and perform and discuss the ethnic music of his or her group. Solicit the assistance of this person in coaching the class in the preparation of some of the ethnic songs. (Elementary level.)

5. Using ethnic music as a background, lead the class in a drawing experience, attempting to capture the mood and significance of the music. This experience may also be conducted with students involved in calisthenics and creative dancing. (Elementary level.)

6. In a unit on vocal music, select composers who are not a part of the Western European tradition, but who have contributed to that tradition, and study and perform their music. The same experience may be conducted with the sonata, chamber music, and the symphony. (Secondary level.)

7. Many musicians espouse a philosophy of freedom, nonviolence, love, patience, endurance, etc., in popular music. Select one musician and based on a number of his or her recordings; aid the class in tracing this particular philosophy. (Secondary level.)

8. Using the encyclopedia, popular trade magazines, and newspaper articles, write the life story and the rise to fame of a popular musician (for example, Santana, Buffy Sainte-Marie, Stevie Wonder, Jose Feliciano, Xavier Cugat) and present research as a musical play, involving several performers to recreate the music. This could be a multimedia presentation, involving music, art, and drama. (Secondary level.)

Arts Curriculum

The following ideas were offered by Horace Clarence Boyer of the University of Massachusetts:

1. Seek out local artists from ethnic groups whose work captures the ethnicity of their group, and request a display of this work in the classroom, hallway, or a suitable place in the school or community. Such persons should also be consulted on approaching other ethnic artists for displays and assistance in creative

work by the class. (Both elementary and secondary levels.)

2. Approach the appropriate budget committee or PTA for funds for the purchase of ethnic prints, copies, and slides of great works of art through companies offering reasonable prices and representative reproductions (such as Lamberts of California, Sietu of Dorchester, Massachusetts, as well as local, state, and national galleries and museums, etc.). (Both elementary and secondary levels.)

3. Encourage local and state galleries and museums to buy, borrow, or rent shows featuring the work of ethnic artists (the National Gallery of Washington, Smithsonian Institute, etc.). (Both elementary and secondary levels.)

4. As a class project, subscribe to *Akwesasne Notes* (available from Mohawk Nation, Rooseveltown, New York, 13683), a Native American newspaper published eight times a year at a contributory fee. This paper not only includes news and editorials of all Native Americans in the United States, but carries lists of resources, poetry, and posters of Native American life. Collect these posters, and mount and display them in the classroom, school hall, or assembly room. (Both elementary and secondary levels.)

5. Conduct a comparative study of the paintings "A Study of Negro Heads" by the Dutch painter, Rembrandt, and "The Card Game" by Horace Pippin, an Afro-American painter, focusing on style, technique, form, color, and craftsmanship. (Both elementary and secondary levels.)

6. Read to the class (or if the class is the third grade or above, have them read) a story of one of the ethnic groups in the United States, and have them attempt to capture the characteristic features of the main characters of the story. Special attention should be given to eyes, nose, mouth, and hair. (Elementary level.)

7. Have the class attempt to reproduce one of the famous paintings discussed above. (Secondary level.)

8. Using those paintings and pieces of sculpture presently owned by the school's art department which reflect our multiracial society, convert the school hallway or assembly room into a gallery, with each picture or piece of sculpture properly identified

and discussed through research by the class. (Secondary level.)

Drama/Theatre Curriculum

The following ideas were offered by Horace Clarence Boyer of the University of Massachusetts:

1. In most secondary schools, the drama club presents two plays each school term. One of the plays might be selected from the classical or Broadway repertoire, and the second should be a play about one of the ethnic groups in the United States. (Secondary level.)

2. Use an integrated cast in plays to assure that characters are believable, regardless of color or nationality. (Both elementary and secondary levels.)

3. Since Spanish is taught in grades one through twelve, combine the efforts of the Spanish class and drama class in the following manner: Ask the Spanish class to translate sections of a play in English into Spanish, or a section of a play in Spanish into English, and have the drama class present the play in the bilingual version. (Secondary level.)

4. As the culminating experience in a unit on an ethnic group, have the class write a play or several short skits exposing the results of the unit, and present the same before other classes or the entire school. If the group selected is a bilingual group, be sure to present a part of the play or skit in the native tongue. (Elementary level.)

5. In preparation for Memorial Day or the Fourth of July, have the class write a play with a representative from each of the ethnic groups in the country explaining how his or her group has contributed to the growth and development of this nation. Include music, dance, and pageantry. (Both elementary and secondary levels.)

6. As an experiment, select a number of plays, essays, and poems by Third World artists as the curriculum for a semester of reading in an English or literature class in grades nine through

eleven. The so-called masterworks would have to be read in grades seven, eight, and twelve. Such a plan would require a year's preparation. (Secondary level.)

7. Ask the music specialist at the school if the annual operetta could be replaced by a number of meaningful skits and musical selections from Third World plays and musicals. One might begin with selections from *The Me Nobody Knows, India, South Pacific*, etc. (Elementary level.)

8. Write a play focusing on the Western Europeans and ethnic groups who were a part of American culture during the first one hundred years of American independence (1776-1876), and select appropriate music to convert the play into a musical. This project could be a multimedia presentation involving music, art, and drama. (Both elementary and secondary levels.)

Modern Language Curriculum

1. In the study of languages, use bilingual magazines and dictionaries, but be sure to emphasize diversity within cultures whose languages are under study. (Not all Hispanics are alike and not all Puerto Ricans are alike).

2. Recognize that culturally-influenced learning styles may be represented in modern language classrooms.

3. Collect artifacts associated with the language under study.

4. Permit persons (students or others) for whom the language under study is a first language to share both artifacts and experiences associated with the cultural dimensions of that language. (There are millions of persons in the United States for whom English is not the first language).

5. Recognize language-culture interface. Also, understand that the traditional modern languages studied in the United States failed to embrace second language acquisition when such acquisition meant academic survival or economic survival.

6. Be sure to hold frequent discussions of stereotypes of the cultures in which the languages are most often used.

7. Please recognize that a multilingual dimension is already

part of the American academic mosaic. How can we make the most of such diversity?

8. Modern language instruction should really embrace the role, scope, and function of bilingual education within a multicultural focus.

9. Language instruction should reflect a clear understanding of the urgency of language learning involvement for refugees and for others for whom English is not a first language.

10. Modern language instruction should reflect a keen understanding of the research associated with second-language acquisition with poor learners.

11. Modern language instruction should embrace a more formal understanding of the work of the U.S. Immigration Services, their positions on aliens, and the perception of the movement to citizenship for new immigrants.

12. Under the multicultural focus, modern language instruction must help to eliminate the image that its purpose is for economically advantaged persons to survive on pleasure trips to other nations.

13. Be sure to discuss how the language of an ethnic group connects with the group's preferences, values, symbols, and priorities.

14. Be sure to discuss the role of nonverbal language and communication in the task of second language acquisition. What can be learned about an ethnic/racial group through the study of language or communication styles?

Library Media Services

Because the transformation of the American school curriculum is underway in the age of information, specialists in library science and learning media services should be aware that the cultural-ethnic demographic trends suggest attention to culturally-influenced learning styles which may demand multiple channels for learning. The nature of information made available and the extent to which diversity represents the collections will indicate much about the program's commitment to equity.

Following are some considerations:

1. What are the cultural-ethnic-gender influences of new library acquisitions? What has been the cross-cultural experiences of those making ultimate decisions about the overall collection?

2. Collections for which populations? Does the librarian assume that the absence of African American children suggests that periodicals like *Ebony* and *Jet* should be omitted from school libraries?

3. Be sure to include works by authentic authors and basic authors in the school's collection.

4. Specialists in library services should understand that today's learner responds very well to sight and sound. The power of television for information acquisition should not be discounted by those offering information services.

5. To what extent are videos, copy machines, interactive video, and previewing space a part of your library?

6. How does the consumer-faculty person communicate to the information specialist (librarians, etc.) about the need for new acquisitions, both print and nonprint?

7. How does a teacher know about new acquisitions?

Agricultural Education Curriculum

1. Much of agricultural education should examine the perspective on instruction with culturally-different populations.

2. Emphasize the significant relationship between poverty and hunger and the contributions of agriculture to eliminating both. Recent reports indicate that hunger is becoming a major problem in the United States, and it continues to be so in less developed countries.

3. Incorporate stories like that of George Washington Carver and peanut farming.

4. Explore nutritional intelligence and its relationship to the field of agriculture, especially with economically poor populations.

5. Incorporate the role, scope, and function of the United States Department of Agriculture (USDA) and its impact on all of us.

6. Emphasize the consumer role of the work of the U. S. Food and Drug Administration.

7. Discuss the role of consumer advocate groups and the function of consumer protection groups or agencies in America.

8. Remember to emphasize the need for increased ethnic literacy both for domestic racial/ethnic populations and those outside the United States.

9. While it is important to help all learners understand that a common element among all groups and cultures is the consumption of food, it should be emphasized that food production patterns relate to climate, culture, and technology of production and distribution.

10. Examine the role and contributions of women in the field of agriculture.

11. What has been the pattern of minority management training in agriculture—especially in agriculture's transition to agribusiness?

Role of Educational Institutions

Because public school is the most common shared experience for most Americans, the United States has depended upon schools to Americanize its citizens. Unfortunately, the focus on schooling in the United States has been primarily on the enhancement of one group's culture and the corresponding neglect of the culture of other groups. Because they have excluded information on the cultures of non-whites in their curricula, schools in the United States have long promoted the view that Nordic Anglo-Saxon superiority exists in all aspects of life, while simultaneously promoting the inherent inferiority of non-Nordic origins of life (Baptiste, 1994).

American schools have become monocultural environments that present only a narrow view of the essence of human experience through the Western Civilization curriculum. By doing so, schools have denied children of color the opportunity to view themselves and their cultures as having value and worth, and have failed to recognize and appreciate the many and varied contributions people of color have made to the dominant culture (Banks, 1991).

Disadvantage in the Educational System

Multicultural education is a process by which individuals and groups can learn to internalize the facts of cultural pluralism to bring about a society that recognizes cultural diversity. Equitable coexistence among the cultural groups that constitute this society is an essential goal.

Steps need to be taken toward achieving educational equity for all groups of students. Historically in this country, children of color and the disadvantaged have not been given equal opportunities in the public educational system. The system has failed to meet their special needs and now should begin to address some of the problems that it has inadvertently, unintentionally, or systematically created or helped to perpetuate.

Funding Practices

Jonathan Kozol (1991) cites the lack of adequate funding for inner-city schools as a source of inequity in the American public school system. According to Kozol, the basic formula for education financing at the state level is the "foundation program." This program allows a local tax to be levied on the homes and businesses within a district to support public education. The same tax rate is issued for both the richest district and the poorest district in the state. Based only on this, inequities occur in the amount of funds available to the respective districts because the value of the homes and businesses in wealthier districts are greater than those in poorer districts. The state, recognizing that the poorer districts may not generate enough money, then provides "sufficient funds to lift the poorer districts to a level (the foundation) roughly equal to that of the richest district" (p. 208). As proposed, this should allow for equalization of all school districts. However, this is not the case.

The states, in order to entice wealthier districts to accept the foundation level, also provide additional funding to the wealthier districts. If this were not enough, usually representatives from the wealthier districts have the major say in determining the foundation. The foundation is not set at the level of the richest district, but rather at a much lower foundation:

> The low foundation is a level of subsistence that will raise a district to a point at which its schools are able to provide a "minimum" or "basic" education, but not an education on the level found in rich districts. (Kozol, 1991, p. 208)

In adhering to the foundation program, many states perpetuate an unequal education system that favors the rich. Use of this school funding process is under increasing fire, and recent state court actions are providing a basis for some change (Kozol, 1991), albeit slow and inadequate.

Monocultural Curriculum

The curriculum poses additional problems for the students of color in the schools. Currently, the curriculum in American schools does not present the cultural views and contributions of people from groups other than the dominant culture (Anglo-American/Eurocentric). It is essential that the curriculum reflect the culturally diverse nation in which we live, so that all students can gain a better appreciation of the diversity that exists.

In the past, white students have appeared to benefit from the Euro-American world view because their culture is attuned to this view. These students have rarely been required to be "bicultural, bilingual, bicognitive" (Pine & Hilliard, 1990, p. 596). However, this is the norm for children of color; they have consistently been required to adapt to the dominant culture.

Racism—Institutional and Otherwise

Another dilemma for students of color is racism. Racism persists at the individual level—there are still those who believe that people of a particular group are inferior based solely on physical traits. Racists think that racial groups other than their own are intellectually, psychologically, and morally inferior.

Racism has also been institutionalized through U.S. laws, judicial decisions, customs, and practices. Often, laws and judicial decisions have supported inequalities among the different ethnic groups. An example is the U.S. Supreme Court decision in *Plessy v. Ferguson* in 1896, which allowed segregation in public schools based on the separate but equal doctrine. This separate but equal approach was later determined to be inherently unequal by the U.S. Supreme Court decision of *Brown v. Board of Education of Topeka* in 1954.

The process of multiculturalism through education will assist all students in their understanding the cultural diversity that comprises our society. Such understanding will help eliminate the racism and discrimination that remain alive and well in U.S. society today.

Through the public school system, the United States has the responsibility and obligation of continuing to pass on the values and beliefs of a democratic society. Because this country was founded on the tenet that all are created equal, all should have equal opportunities and equal access to a better life. If schools embrace the concepts of cultural pluralism, members of all groups will benefit.

Current Trends
in Multicultural Education

Much of the current literature on multicultural education recognizes the importance of the preparation of educational leaders and teachers for culturally diverse schools and classrooms. Multicultural education cannot and will not be successful without principals and teachers who are able to provide both the environment and the instruction conducive to the goals of multiculturalism. The literature suggests that administrators and future teachers need to be prepared to address both the educational and the cultural needs of their students (Reed, 1992; Ford, 1992; and Kraig, 1992). Three major areas are identified as critical for future and current principals and teachers:

1. Preparation for the teaching of language minority students;

2. Recognition of the learning styles of culturally different students; and

3. High expectations for culturally different students.

These concepts are not new to educational leadership and teacher education programs, but they have not generally been associated with helping to accomplish the goals of multicultural education.

1. Teaching Language Minority Students

The recruitment and preparation of teachers for language minority students has become increasingly more important given the recent estimates on the number of language minority children in our schools. Garcia (1991) reports that the estimates range from 1.3 to 3.6 million such students. According to him, the divergence in the estimates is caused by the procedures used to obtain the count of language minority children.

Of the total number of language minority students in the United States, the majority have Spanish language backgrounds. Projections for the year 2000 suggest that the proportion of children in the United States with Spanish language background will be about 77 percent of the total number of language minority children in U.S. schools (Garcia, 1991).

All of these students will require some type of bilingual education programs. Garcia notes that several possible programs exist for the language minority students: Transitional Bilingual Education, Maintenance Bilingual Education, English as a Second Language, Immersion, Sheltered English, and Submersion. The types of programs selected must meet the needs of the language minority population in a particular school district. The most critical component of the bilingual education program is the training of the classroom teacher. These educators must be taught to be supportive of the languages and cultures of their students.

2. Recognizing Diverse Learning Styles

University educational leadership and teacher-training programs as well as in-service programs for those teachers currently working in schools must provide information about the various teaching and learning styles. Style differences reasonably occur among administrators, teachers, and students and also between the students and the curriculum. Anderson (1988) has discussed the two basic cognitive styles—field-dependent and field-independent—as they relate to the learning styles of various ethnic groups. In his research, he cites several studies on the differences in ethnic groups.

Field-dependent learners tend to prefer to learn in groups and to interact with the teacher. They may require more extrinsic reinforcement and more structure from the teacher in terms of organization of learning experiences. *Field-independent stu-*

dents appear to be able to respond better to independent and individualized instruction. Unlike field-dependent students, they are more likely to respond to intrinsic motivation (Witkin, Moore, & MacDonald, 1974).

Also of importance is the orientation of the teacher. *Field-independent teachers* prefer a relaxed teaching situation with the instructional emphasis on cognitive or theoretical issues while *field-dependent teachers* are more comfortable with class discussions and interaction with students. Witkin *et. al.* (1974) provide additional information about the learning and teaching styles of field-dependent and field-independent individuals.

The key issue with learning and teaching styles is that teachers must be able to identify the methods of instruction that best suit the learning styles of their students. Differences in learning styles should not be misunderstood and thereby lead to discriminatory practices but rather should be utilized to help students reach their full potential (Bowen & Bowen, 1992).

3. Maintaining High Expectations

Principals should recognize that the attitude of the teacher is paramount not only in accomplishing the goals of multicultural education but also for the educational success of students. Studies have consistently shown that students of teachers not motivated to teach and who have low expectations for their students do not perform as well academically as students whose teachers have high expectations (Good, 1981).

Tracking is a form of teacher-expectation for students. According to Good and Brophy (1990), teacher-expectations have a direct relationship to the tracking system, which is used in many schools. Teachers in the Good and Brophy study who taught low-track classes showed less initiative and creativity in their teaching. Good and Brophy also present studies that suggest that most teachers prefer to teach high-track classes and that those teachers tend to emphasize more higher order thinking skills.

Principals and teachers must begin with positive attitudes

toward their minority students and respect them as individuals. Too often, principals and teachers use varying student backgrounds as an explanation or excuse for poor achievement instead of raising the level of expectation for students. Teachers must demand maximum effort from all students, regardless of race, gender, religion, social economic status, or physical abilities— and they must accept no less.

If teachers are to be successful in the education of culturally different students, they must communicate their expectations to students, show an interest in the students' culture, and establish objectives that are descriptive of learning outcomes and always clear and understandable. Teachers and principals should use positive reinforcement often and continually to let the students know how well they are doing in class. Principals can do this both directly and by example.

For Further Thought

1. What is meant by institutionalizing curriculum?

2. What is meant by preserving the dignity of children in a multicultural society? Cite instances where a child's dignity has been assaulted. Why is it still necessary to remind professionals working with children to preserve their dignity?

3. Please describe six behaviors (on the part of educators) that you would consider to be culturally responsive in instructional delivery. Then cite six behaviors that you consider not culturally responsive.

4. Choose a subject matter area (English, mathematics, social studies, music, etc.) and add ten additional ideas for the practical multicultural transformation of the curriculum. Please number each idea separately.

5. What is a language minority child? How would you respond to those who deny bilingual education and English as a Second Language instruction as a legitimate aspect of American schooling? Cite three main ideas.

6. What is the difference between field dependent learning style and field independent learning style?

References Cited

Anderson, J.A. (1988). Cognitive styles and multicultural populations. *Journal of Teacher Education* 5, 2-9.

Banks, J.A. (1991). *Teaching strategies for ethnic studies*. Boston, MA: Allyn & Bacon.

Baptiste, Jr., H.P. (1994). The multicultural environment of schools: Implications to leaders. In L.W. Hughes, (Ed.), *The Principal as leader*. New York: Merrill/MacMillan, 89-104.

Bowen, D.N. & Bowen, E.A. (1992). Multicultural education: The learning style aspect. In Grant, C.A. (Ed.), *Toward education that is multicultural: Proceedings of the first annual meeting of the National Association for Multicultural Education*. Morristown, NJ: Silver Burdett Ginn, 266-276.

Ford, B. (1992). Developing teachers with a multicultural perspective: A challenge and a mission. In Grant, C.A. (Ed.), *Toward education that is multicultural: Proceedings of the first annual meeting of the National Association for Multicultural Education*. Morristown, NJ: Silver Burdett Ginn, 132-138.

Garcia, R.L. (1991). *Teaching in a pluralistic society: Concepts, models, strategies*. New York: HarperCollins.

Good, T.L. (1981). Teacher expectations and student perceptions: A decade of research. *Educational Leadership*, 38 (5), 415-422.

Good, T.L. & Brophy, J. (1990). *Educational psychology: A realistic approach*, 4th edition. New York: Longman.

Kozol, J. (1991). *Savage inequalities: Children in America's schools*. New York: Crown.

Kraig, G.M. (1992). Implementation of a multicultural education in teacher training program. In Grant, C.A. (Ed.), *Toward education that is multicultural: Proceedings of the first annual meeting of the National Association for Multicultural Education*. Morristown, NJ: Silver Burdett Ginn, 139-147.

Pine, G.J. & Hilliard, A.G. (1990). Rx for racism: Imperatives for America's schools. *Phi Delta Kappan*, 71 (8), 593-600.

Reed, D.F. (1992). Preparing teachers for multicultural classrooms. In Grant, C.A. (Ed.), *Toward education that is multicultural: Proceedings of the first annual meeting of the National Association for Multicultural Education*. Morristown, NJ: Silver Burdett Ginn.

Witkin, H.A., Moore, C.A., & MacDonald, F.J. (1974). *Cognitive style and the teaching / learning processes*. (Cassette Series 3F). Washington, DC: American Educational Research Association.

Other References

Baker, G.C. (1994). *Planning and organizing for multicultural instruction*. Menlo Park, CA: Addison-Wesley.

Fiske, E.B. (1991). *Smart schools, smart kids*. New York: Simon & Schuster.

Sadker, M.P. & Sadker, D.M. (1982). *Sex equity handbook for school*. New York: Longman.

Tiedt, P.L. & Tiedt, I.M. (1995). *Multicultural teaching: A handbook of activities, information and resources*. Boston, MA: Allyn & Bacon.

Notes

Harmony
        comes from
                Differences
        not Similarities.

—H. Prentice Baptiste, Jr.
(modified from Rosa Guerreo)

Chapter 6

Baptiste's Typology of Multiculturalism

Internalizing Multiculturalism: A Typology for the Learning Environment

The educational system is composed of various educational environments. Each educational environment has key personnel who are responsible for the climate of that environment. The various educational environments include classrooms/teachers; schools/principals; districts/central office administrators; principal and teacher education programs/professors; and governmental agencies/politicians. Multiculturalism, in order to be successful, requires internalization at the individual, group, and institutional levels.

Baptiste first proposed a typology of multicultural education in 1983 (Baptiste, 1983). Since then, he has further developed and refined his typology of multiculturalism (Baptiste & Archer, 1994). It is his hypothesis that the internalization of multiculturalism in an educational environment or agent can occur on one of at least three conceptual levels. A distinct set of characteristics identify the conceptual level of multiculturalism the educational environment has reached.

The levels in this typology are distinct, each level having parameters that define its specific characteristics. The typology takes into consideration qualitative as well as quantitative differences with respect to the levels of multiculturalism. The qualitative differentiation has three levels—product, process, and philosophical orientation—which show the type and content of integration of multiculturalism. Each level similarly shows a quantitative differentiation.

All formal educational processes will display the same basic components when functioning at Level One of the typology. Keep in mind that there are two parts—*i.e.*, environments (classrooms) as well as personnel (teachers). Thus, a classroom will function at a certain level because the teacher is operating at that level of the typology.

Internalization of multiculturalism is an evolutionary process. There are two aspects to the evolution in an educational environment—quantitative and qualitative. Quantitative measures of the educational environment considered in the typology show that environments differ in the following categories:

- ◆ number of cultural/ethnic groups;
- ◆ number of workshops, courses, or activities devoted to multiculturalism;
- ◆ ethnic/cultural make-up of faculty and students;
- ◆ amount of funds allocated for the multicultural program.

The qualitative dimensions of multiculturalism in the typology are these:

- ◆ product;
- ◆ process;
- ◆ philosophical orientation.

Without internalization of the qualitative dimension, the

prescriptive goals of multiculturalism cannot be achieved.

Level One

This level is characterized as additive and tangible. Multicultural education is manifested as single-focused events, such as cultural celebrations, ethnic-specific courses, and unrelated cultural topics added at various times to the regular curriculum (see Figure 1). Sleeter and Grant (1987) identified approaches to multicultural education in which teaching the culturally different, human relations, and the single-group studies all qualify as Level One of the typology.

Figure 1
Level One Product

Characteristics:
Single focus, additive, tangible.
Cultural celebrations limited to students of color.

Programs:
Cultural differences limited to students of color or minority students.
Human relations: Promote positive self image; usually in elementary schools, schools undergoing desegregation.
Single group studies: Emphasis on one ethnic, racial, or cultural group; geared toward ethnic studies, intent is "quick fix."

Culturally Different Groups

Teaching about culturally different groups by educators is the method most widely used by those people who realize that they are not meeting the needs of their students of color (Sleeter & Grant, 1987). According to Baptiste (1994), these educational efforts are functioning at Level One of internalizing the concepts of multiculturalism. That is to say, they recognize the need to help students of color (African Americans, Asian Americans, Native Americans, and Hispanic Americans) become competent in the culture of the majority group while simultaneously learning about, maintaining, and feeling pride in their own cultures. Educators at this level stress individual achievement and social mobility, but they fail to focus on the underlying problems resulting from the fact that the majority race has dominated capitalism in this society. They do not address the issues surrounding unequal access to goods and services. They are mainly concerned with race and ethnicity only.

Programs instituted at this level are shallow, dealing only with special occasions or events. No attempt is made to effect any sweeping curricular changes. The emphasis is on adding activities to the lessons. At this level, the programs are limited to students of color. Unfortunately, in schools and districts where little or no racial diversity exists, even this limited approach is often deemed unnecessary.

Programs involved at this level may show a strong commitment to the educational needs and the overall welfare of children of color. However, because they are an additive approach, they usually try to address issues in a broad manner instead of being more specific. An example is the use of the term *Hispanic* to identify all children of Spanish heritage or surname, while in reality students whose first language is Spanish come from many different countries and cultures (Mexico, Cuba, Puerto Rico, Argentina, and many others). The same applies to the term *Asian*, which with similar lack of precision is used to treat Japanese, Chinese, Korean, Vietnamese, Laotian, Cambodian, East Indians, and others as one group. Students must be identified as to their specific origin because teaching strategies and learning styles differ among such cultural groups.

A weakness of programs that operate on Level One of the typology lies in the fact that educators using this approach tend to rely on these programs exclusively. They ignore or are not aware of other models of multicultural education. Because these programs are multicultural education for children of color, those who use these methods do not feel it necessary to broaden their scope to include a multicultural process that emphasizes the necessity of exposing all children to the cultural diversities that exist in the United States.

Groups at Level One have a commitment to students of color who have been denied access to full participation in the educational system because of language or cultural difference. They promote a method that implies that these children of color should learn to adapt to a different culture, and, unfortunately, the method does not require that those in the dominant culture make any changes or learn anything about other cultures. The burden is, as it has always been, on those in the minority to change in some way to accommodate the majority. The only difference between the programs on this level and the *cultural assimilation approach* (the process by which an individual or group acquires the culture traits of a different ethnic group) is that people of color are allowed to maintain their own cultural heritage while learning about the new culture.

Human Relations

The goal of Level One programs for recognizing the cultural diversity that exists is to assist students of different cultural backgrounds to communicate and get along with each other. Another aim is to promote a positive self-image so that students feel good about themselves.

These programs are usually introduced in elementary schools. They support the use of nonstereotypical materials and activities that promote interaction among the different groups. Schools addressing problems of desegregation generally try to implement this approach because it emphasizes ideas and suggestions about how to help students understand cultural differences between and among their classmates.

One of the reasons this approach is placed in Level One of the typology is that after communication and understanding between the groups have been achieved, this approach has no other agenda—it identifies no other problems to be addressed. No effort is made to deal with other problems that militate against the achievement of a culturally pluralistic society. Unless other problems are addressed, a culturally pluralistic society will not be achieved.

Single-Group Studies

The single-group method of multicultural programming places its emphasis on one racial, ethnic, or cultural group. This approach is geared toward ethnic studies. This Level One approach may identify one or more specific ethnic groups to be included as units of study—an additive approach.

Perhaps the most salient characteristics of all Level One programs are their reactive posture and lack of institutionalization. In these programs, tangibles are used to suggest something other than the real intent of the program. Often, the cultural/ ethnic emphases are for specific populations and are limited geographically. Usually the catalyst for initiating these programs is external pressure brought about by interest groups, social pressure, or community ethnic groups. The intent is a quick fix to the problem without real change to existing programs or policies.

Level Two

Qualitative differences exist between Levels One and Two. At Level Two in the typology, a confluent relationship exists between product and process. In Level Two efforts, the tangible products are embedded in a matrix of process. Programs at this level possess a theoretical referent link with practical applications, allowing multiculturalism to take on a broader base as it is incorporated into the infrastructure of the institution.

At Level Two, multicultural concepts are integrated into all educational components. For example, the curriculum is restructured to include various cultural and ethnic perspectives on topics, events, and concepts. Generic components of multicultural education and strategies for incorporating them are identified for implementation. Additionally, steps are taken to institutionalize various facets of multiculturalism. Specific courses and related experiences are formalized within the program. A broad conceptual framework is formed at this level, one that guides the amalgamation of the principles and goals of multiculturalism with the other components of the educational programs.

Figure 2
Level Two Process/Product

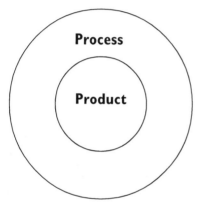

Characteristics:
Confluent relationship between product and process.
Theoretical referent link with practical applications.
Curriculum restructured to include various cultural and ethnic perspectives.
Steps taken to institutionalize various facets of multiculturalism.
Broad conceptual framework formed to guide amalgamation of multiculturalism with education programs.

Programs:
Cultural diversity approach: Understanding of culture and its parameters; moves toward institutionalizing cultural diversity as both product and process.

Cultural Diversity Approach

The cultural diversity approach to multicultural education is included in Level Two of the typology. Those who incorporate this approach begin by gaining an understanding of culture and its parameters. Next, they acquire knowledge about the contributions of ethnic, racial, and cultural groups to society in the United States.

Discussions of gender and social class are included in the activities of programs using the cultural diversity approach. At Level Two, care is taken not to replace one type of human diversity with another (*i.e.*, sexism or classism does not become a substitute for racism). One of the concerns with this approach revolves around the controversy regarding other diversities. Many programs do not include gender, class, or handicap in their approach to multiculturalism. This is limiting because these factors may be interrelated with race and ethnicity and therefore deserving of inclusion in this approach.

The cultural diversity approach has other limitations. It does emphasize culture, but, as with the programs of Level One, it fails to deal with social stratification. By excluding such issues, educators send the message that the important aspect of multicultural education is only to allow culturally different groups to maintain and value their cultural differences. This cultural diversity approach does go beyond those of Level One by moving toward institutionalizing multiculturalism as both a product and a process.

Level Three

Achievement of Level Three in the typology is accomplished only after successful completion of Level Two. Level Three represents a highly sophisticated internalization of the process of multiculturalism and the added dimension of a philosophical orientation that permeates the educational environment. This pervasive quality causes the educational institution to respond to its mission and goals in a manner consistent with the conceptualized principles and goals of genuine multiculturalism.

In order to achieve Level Three status, an educational institution must emerge from the product stage of Level One and the combination product/process stage of Level Two to a sophisticated and regenerative conceptualized knowledge base for multiculturalism.

The goals of Level Three programs are extended to help students "gain a better understanding of the causes of oppression and inequality and ways in which these social problems might be eliminated" (Suzuki, 1984, p. 308). Activities at this level point to the unequal inclusiveness of various groups in American society, exploring and examining the underlying reasons. At Level Three, cultural diversity is regarded as an asset rather than a problem, and the appreciation of diversity is used to progress toward a culturally pluralistic society.

A philosophy based on the principles of equality, recognition and respect of human diversity, and a sense of moral commitment serves as the blueprint for the emergence of a multicultural process which leads to cultural pluralism.

> Although the legitimacy of multiculturalism is no longer a question, debatable issues do exist. These issues serve to further the refinement and expansion of knowledge from new perspectives. Finally, this level has a matureness in conceptualization, rationalization, and direction. (Baptiste & Baptiste, 1980, p. 44)

Administrators and other educators operating at this level have internalized a philosophy of the basic tenets of multiculturalism that provides them with support and a commitment to action. They are social activists.

Figure 3
Level Three—Philosophical Orientation

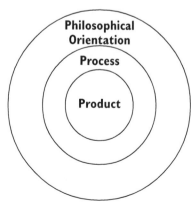

Philosophical Orientation
Process
Product

Characteristics:

A philosophy permeated by the principles of equality; recognition of and respect for human diversity; values that support cultural diversity.
All children valued.

All pedagogy restructured or reconstituted to exemplify the basic tenets of multiculturalism.
Cultural diversity regarded as an asset not a problem.
A moral commitment to social action for equity.

Programs:

There are no specific identifiable programs operating at this level.

Figure 4—Typology of Multiculturalization

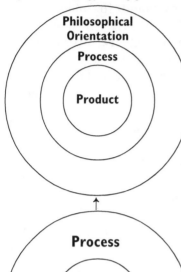

Level 3 Process/Philosophical Orientation

Characteristics:

A philosophy permeated by the principles of equality; recognition of and respect for human diversity; values that support cultural diversity.

All children valued.

All pedagogy restructured or reconstituted to exemplify the basic tenets of multiculturalism.

Cultural diversity regarded as an asset not a problem.

A moral commitment to social action for equity.

Programs:

There are no specific identifiable programs operating at this level.

Level 2 Process/Product

Characteristics:

Confluent relationship between product and process.

Theoretical referent link with practical applications.

Curriculum restructured to include various cultural and ethnic perspectives.

Steps taken to institutionalize various facets of multiculturalism.

Broad conceptual framework formed to guide amalgamation of multiculturalism with education programs.

Programs:

Cultural diversity approach: Understanding of culture and its parameters; moves toward institutionalizing cultural diversity as both product and process.

Level 1 Product

Characteristics:

Single focus, additive, tangible.

Cultural celebrations limited to students of color.

Programs:

Cultural differences limited to students of color or minority students.

Human relations: Promote positive self image; usually in elementary schools, schools undergoing desegregation.

Single group studies: Emphasis on one ethnic, racial, or cultural group; geared toward ethnic studies, intent is "quick fix."

Figure 5—
Typology for Multiculturalizing Science Instruction

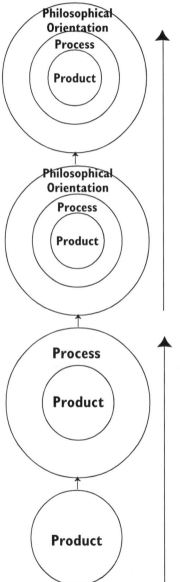

Level 3 Process/Philosophical Orientation

Commitment to the philosophy of multicultural science education. Science program permeated by the philosophy of multiculturalism, both formal and informal activities are reflective of science instruction that is multicultural. Science instruction is non-elitist.

Level 2 Process/Product

Infusion of diverse cultural perspectives and contributions to a science concept development and/or evolvement. Minority and women scientists' experiences and contributions are tied into the teaching of science concepts and topics. Science instruction is commensurate with diverse learning and cognititve styles. Problem solving processes and scientific method utilized in elucidating the faultiness of racial and sexual stereotypes, prejudices, and ethnocentrism. Contextual array of science content is permeated with diversity.

Level 1 Product

Focus on minority and women scientists' contributions in isolation. Highlighting an ethnic or cultural group invention, discovery, or contribution or minority scientist's birthday.

Figure 6—Typology
for Multiculturalizing Mathematics Instruction

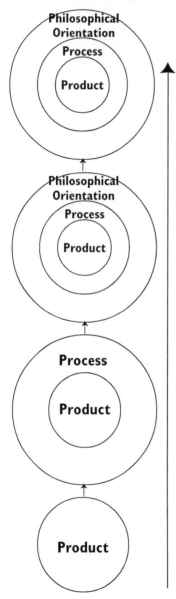

Level 3 Process/Philosophical Orientation

Commitment to the philosophy of multicultural mathematics education. Mathematics program permeated by the philosophy of multiculturalism; both formal and informal activities are reflective of mathematics instruction that is multicultural. Mathematics instruction is non-elitist.

Level 2 Process/Product

Infusion of diverse cultural perspectives and contributions to a mathematics concept development and/or evolvement. Minority and women mathematicians' experiences and contributions are tied into the teaching of mathematics concepts and topics. Mathematics instruction is commensurate with diverse learning and cognititve styles. Problem solving processes and mathematics logic and reasoning utilized in elucidating the faultiness of racial and sexual stereotypes, prejudices, and ethnocentrism. Contextual array of mathematics content is permeated with diversity.

Level I Product

Focus on minority and women mathematicians' contributions in isolation. Highlighting an ethnic or cultural group invention, discovery, or contribution or minority mathematician's birthday.

Figure 7—Typology for Multiculturalizing Early Childhood Education

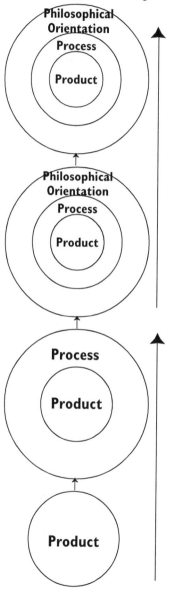

Level 3 Process/Philosophical Orientation

Commitment to the philosophy of multiculturalizing early childhood educational programs. Activities and teaching strategies promote positive self-esteem in young children, thus enabling the development of self-empowerment and positive group identity. Educational environment is replete with anti-bias resources that proactively guide young children in social responsible cross-cultural behavior. Cultural diversity is an asset. All Children are valued

Level 2 Process/Product

Cultural experiences are developmentally appropriate for target population. Ethnically and culturally diverse resources and materials characterizes all educational curriculum and teaching strategies. Concepts (*e.g.,* family, body parts, skin color, etc.) are introduced using various cultural perspectives.

Level 1 Product

Activities focus on single cultural/ethnic group. Celebrations of ethnic holidays and ethnic dances. Exotic or stereotypical portrayal of cultural parameters of various cultural groups are prevalent. Additive unrelated cultural activities are routine.

Figure 8—Typology
for Multiculturalization of Residency Program

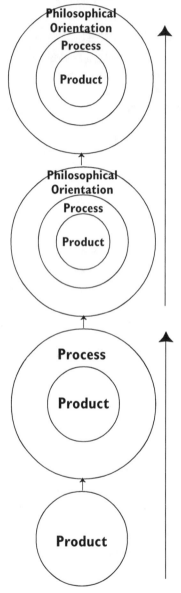

Level 3 Process/Philosophical Orientation

Moral commitment to serving the urban underserved populations. Social activist orientation by residents for patients and their community. No "Tuskeegee Experiments." At this level, the traditional doctor/patient relationship is replaced by the culturally diverse ethos of doctor/client or doctor/consumer relationship that attributes mutual respect and parity shared decision-making regarding treatment. Faculty and staff fully committed to an infusion of a multicultural philosophy into the curriculum.

Level 2 Process/Product

Mission statement includes the preparation of residents to effectively serve culturally diverse and underserved populations. Comprehensive plan with theoretical referent for internalizing various cultural and ethnic perspectives. Anthropological, sociological, and psychological concerns are on parity with biochemical concerns in residency training. Strategies to facilitate and improve cross-cultural communication have been formalized as an integral part of the residency program.

Level I Product

Hit/miss mode of operation for inclusion of cultural and ethnic perspectives in residency curriculum. Susceptibility of certain cultural or ethnic groups to various diseases, illnesses, or ailments—*e.g.,* sickle cell anemia, hypertension (Blacks), alcoholism (Native Americans), diabetes, mellitus/hypertension for Mexican-Americans.

Cross-Cultural Communication

The fundamental concept underlying the development of the methodologies, programs, and theories in cross-cultural communication is that the values, behaviors, beliefs, and assumptions of one's own culture must be brought to a conscious awareness before effective interaction with persons from other cultures is possible. Another basic concept is that the examination of cultural differences is valid on several accounts. As Barna and Jain (1978) wrote, cultural differences are useful for purposes of contrast so as to bring one's own cultural background into awareness.

Secondly, it is assumed that cultural differences affect various aspects of the communication process and therefore need to be understood fully in order to communicate more effectively. This assumption lead Stewart to state, "The overall goal of cross-cultural training is to provide a framework within which people can develop skills and acquire the knowledge that increases their ability to function effectively in a bi- or multicultural environment and to derive satisfaction from the intercultural experience" (cited in Pusch 1979, p. 95).

These assumptions have led to an emphasis on the development of training programs that could efficiently and quickly give people new communication skills so that they can be more effective in their jobs overseas or, in the case of international students, are able to take full advantage of any educational experience. As a result, we find extensive development of methodology over the last several decades.

Cross-Cultural Methods

These methodologies include the simulation method, role plays, case studies/critical incidents, and Contrast American. The simulation method involves some type of game in which individuals play the role of either mock cultures or of cultures other than their own and act out certain scenarios. The intent of the simulation is for the participants to "experience" going to another culture, ethnocentrism, and cultural isolation in a controlled environment. The facilitator then guides the debriefing so that participants can acknowledge their feelings and reactions and notice the similarity to actual cross-cultural experiences.

While there are a number of simulations, *Bafa Bafa*, designed by Shirts (1973), is one of the most well-known. Hoopes and Ventura (1979) were among the early developers of Contrast American methods in which lists of American values/behaviors are examined and then contrasted with the opposite values/ behaviors, thereby enabling the participants to evaluate their own cultural and/or individual values and behaviors as being on a continuum between the two. Brislin *et al.'s* (1986) cultural assimilator takes a critical incident—an occurrence between individuals from differing cultures in which they have different behaviors—and expands on it, culminating with four possible explanations for the different behavior. The participant has to choose one of the explanations. Each of the four choices is then explained as to whether it is more or less probable.

Role playing is normally used so that participants can try out the behavior of another culture to develop a new personal behavior that is more appropriate for dealing with another culture. Case studies are similar in that they are a written example of a culture conflict or problem which the participants have to try to resolve. All of these methods emphasize experiential learning because research shows such learning to be most effective in enabling students to acquire useful knowledge of other cultures.

Cross-Cultural Programs

There have been three basic kinds of programs for cross-culture communication. Two have been almost exclusively in the field of business—the predeparture orientation and re-entry programs. Predeparture orientation programs have been designed for individuals (mostly American) going to live in other countries, giving the Americans information about the new culture as well as seeking to develop the process of communication. Re-entry programs have been designed for individuals returning from overseas assignments to assist them in re-adapting to their native culture as quickly as possible.

A third program, Intercultural Communication Workshops (ICW), has more relevance for this chapter. An ICW can last from one week to one semester and has three basic sequential parts. The first part introduces the concepts of culture and attendant aspects such as ethnocentrism, stereotyping, and communication. The second part emphasizes self-awareness and values clarification, while the third section introduces culture specific information (see Figure 9). The progression of the ICW is from low risk activities to high risk, from highly structured to less

Figure 9:
Intercultural Communication Workshop Model

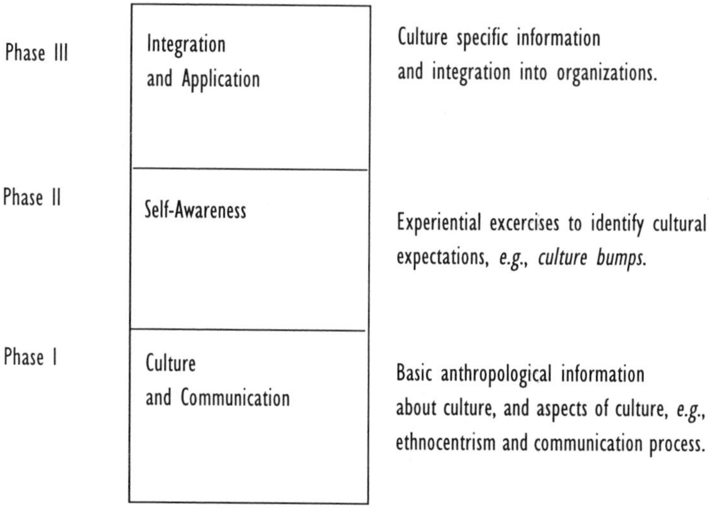

Phase III	Integration and Application	Culture specific information and integration into organizations.
Phase II	Self-Awareness	Experiential excercises to identify cultural expectations, *e.g., culture bumps.*
Phase I	Culture and Communication	Basic anthropological information about culture, and aspects of culture, *e.g.,* ethnocentrism and communication process.

structured. The ICW has been used extensively in business training in corporations that have employees of differing cultural backgrounds (especially between American and Saudi employees during the 1970s) and has also been used in preparing international students for their sojourn in the United States. It was in this latter capacity that the *culture bump* was developed.

Culture Bumps

The culture bump is a concept that incorporates a number of the methods outlined above. We can understand better the origin of the culture bump if we look at the nature of stereotyping according to Brislin (1981). While he outlines four basic functions or reasons for people developing prejudice and stereotypes, it is only the knowledge function that is relevant to the proposal in this chapter. Brislin says that the knowledge function explains one reason for the development of stereotypes and prejudices. According to this concept, stereotypes and prejudices allow people to explain the world around them to themselves. He further states that this category is derived more from common sense than scholarly literature and recommends that more attention be given to this common, but heretofore neglected, type of everyday prejudice. The systematic examination of culture bumps is an attempt to do so.

According to Archer (1990), a culture bump refers to those incidents in which an individual has expectations of a particular behavior from other people in a particular situation but receives different behavior from individuals who are culturally different. Simply put, it is a cultural difference—or a critical incident. When people have culture bumps, they experience a break in the feeling of affiliation with the other individual. The normal reaction is to try and reconnect, usually by seeking to understand *them*. The inquiry stems from a *why* basis, *e.g.*: "Why do they...?" However, if we analyze the question: "Why do they...?" we find that embedded in it is another question: "Why do they not do these things the way we do them?" or, more succinctly: "Why are they different from us?" Unfortunately, any answer that is given will now reinforce the sense of separation that prompted the question in the first place. With the best of intentions, the person now has perhaps gained information about *them*, but has actually lost the relationship with *them*.

This strategy reinforces cultural differences and thwarts attempts to find universal similarities. The culture bump methodology allows the individual to intervene at the original incident and analyze it in a different way that leads to a different question: "How do *they* express...?" and embedded in this question is the more fundamental question of "How do *they* do what we do?" and "How are we the same?" This inquiry guides the individual to an affective understanding of the concept that we are fundamentally the same yet different culturally. By experiencing that our differences are cultural rather than personal, the individuals feel that they are two human beings sitting side by side looking *out at* their cultural differences, rather than two individuals sitting across from one another looking *at* their differences.

Some examples of culture bumps include a Puerto Rican child lowering his eyes when being scolded, a Vietnamese student offering to use his influence to help his professor at City Hall, a Mexican American teacher standing beside the desk of a White student and touching him on the shoulder, a White teacher using her first name in a class that includes Indochinese students, an African American student looking at the desk while her teacher speaks to her, American-born teachers putting students from Cuba in small discussion groups, or an African American student coming into the classroom after the class has begun and greeting the teacher as she does so. The specific steps in analyzing any culture bump are as follows:

1. Pinpoint the culture bump.
2. Define the universal situation.
3. List the behavior of the other individual.
4. List your own behavior.

5. List your feelings.
6. List the behavior you expect from people of your own group in that particular situation.
7. What is the quality the particular behavior represents for you?
8. How do people in the other culture express that particular quality?

Upon completion of the steps, the individual with the bump discovers that he does not know what he thought he knew about the other individual. It reveals to him his ignorance and places him in a position to eliminate the ignorance so now he can find the answer to the question that he did not know he had. The process emphasizes the importance of observing behavior in objective language without judgment and the importance of acknowledging one's own feelings—negative as well as positive. Then by analyzing one's own expectations, the individual discovers his own cultural beingness.

While validating one's own culture, the process simultaneously legitimatizes other ways of reacting in a universal situation existing among human beings everywhere. The process provides a language with which to talk about differences without being personal or judgmental of others or of self. For example, to say, "I had a negative (or positive or neutral) culture bump," is accurate and concise. Furthermore, the responsibility for the incident now rests with the appropriate person.

Using Cross-Cultural Communication in Multicultural Education

As can be seen in the overview presented above, we have two similar disciplines developing side by side, but with some critical distinctions. Those distinctions have at times separated them in the past, but may now become mutual strengths as the two disciplines begin to work toward a common goal. The logical place for their convergence is at the point of inception—in the preparation of the teacher for a multicultural educational experience. It can be seen that both multicultural education and cross-cultural communication have strengths and weaknesses. Multicultural education has defined system relations, such as power and political influences. It has also defined exactly what a multicultural educational system is and how it should function in addition to developing historical and cultural definitions of various ethnic groups in the United States. It has been less successful in its ability to implement its ideas.

Cross-cultural communication has focused on methodology and implementation, yet has not dealt with systematic relationships and historical injustices and oppression of individuals or of groups. Neither group has emphasized commonalities between groups although such a resolution is the implicit goal of both.

After having examined the two disciplines, let us now look at the possibility of blending the two together. This potential was acknowledged by Stewart in a 1973 speech when he stated:

> Cross-cultural training is an affirming experience and this affirmation works to reinforce the role and position of minority groups in a pluralistic society. It functions to reduce tensions and build bridges among people of different cultural backgrounds. It also places heavy stress on the learning potential available in intercultural encounters, ways of taking advantage of those opportunities and the acceptance of cultural diversity as a human resource rather than merely as an impediment to communication.

This is not a new idea, as multicultural education has always used some methodology from cross-cultural communication, but what has been missing is a comprehensive model for the integration of the two disciplines. We will now propose an integration of cross-cultural communication and the various approaches to multicultural education. Specifically, the teacher should receive a basic education in three areas:

Factual information—about various cultures, including their own. Americans, for example, do not study American culture, except tangentially in sociology class. Neither do we study, except in special cases, such as multicultural education classes, Arab American, Hispanic American, or African American cultures.

Experiences—actual, field-based experiences with people from one's own and other cultures. Teacher candidates should have a structured, multicultural experience in which they are mentored by one or more experienced teachers. This multicultural internship differs from practice teaching which focuses on other aspects of the teaching process. This is an internship in which teacher candidates are specifically dealing with two or more cultures.

Meta-experience—This allows the students to acknowledge, analyze, and seek feedback and other interpretations from their actual experience with other cultures. This experiential learning is critical for an integration of the other two types of learning. In fact, without this type of learning, the other two can actually reinforce stereotypes of people from other cultures.

One way to visualize the sequencing of the progression is to superimpose an Intercultural Communication Workshop (ICW) on the Typology of Multiculturalization in a horizontal fashion. Thus, we can see that at Level One, there is an emphasis on learning about culture, acknowledging differences in culture, and acquiring the skill of effectively communicating cross culturally. At Level Two, there is an emphasis on self-awareness; and at Level Three, the curriculum emphasizes integration of the first two levels with application. Now let us look in more detail at each level of the typology (See Figure 10).

Figure 10: Comprehensive Multicultural Teacher Preparation Program (Merging of Multiculturalism and Intercultural Communication Models)

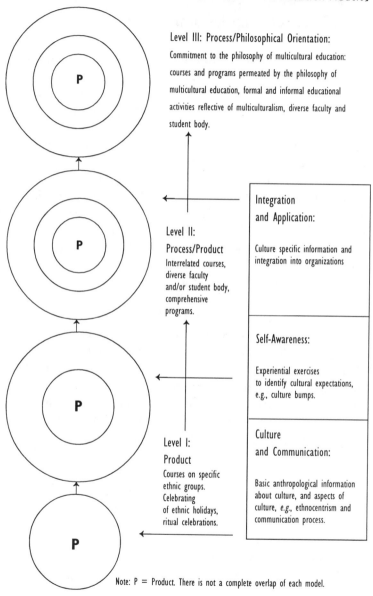

Level III: Process/Philosophical Orientation:
Commitment to the philosophy of multicultural education: courses and programs permeated by the philosophy of multicultural education, formal and informal educational activities reflective of multiculturalism, diverse faculty and student body.

Integration and Application:

Culture specific information and integration into organizations

Level II: Process/Product
Interrelated courses, diverse faculty and/or student body, comprehensive programs.

Self-Awareness:

Experiential exercises to identify cultural expectations, e.g., culture bumps.

Level I: Product
Courses on specific ethnic groups. Celebrating of ethnic holidays, ritual celebrations.

Culture and Communication:

Basic anthropological information about culture, and aspects of culture, e.g., ethnocentrism and communication process.

Note: P = Product. There is not a complete overlap of each model.

119

The Typology Levels
and Intercultural Communication

Starting with the definition of Level One, we encounter curriculum that is product oriented and represents an additive approach with a single focus on ethnic celebrations and lacking any contextual reference. The question then becomes, how can cross-cultural sequencing and methodology be applied to move this curriculum closer to a Level Two? Since, the minimal level has been achieved through external pressure, the cross-cultural truism of beginning with low risk and gradually moving to higher risk activities would be well heeded at this point. The two approaches to multicultural education, outlined by Sleeter and Grant (1987) and referred to earlier in this section, would be appropriate at this level. In addition, at this level several cross-cultural methodologies would be useful in moving you toward Level Two. Cultural assimilators and case studies are both very effective at this level. They are low-risk yet begin the process of having the teacher start accepting cultural differences.

The next step would be to introduce simulations which are still a low-risk activity, as a means for individuals to examine their bias in interacting with people who are "different." In addition, the simulations begin to move the teachers and others toward a more process-oriented cultural learning style. A particularly effective method would be American Contrast exercises. Since these are most effective when conducted with ethnically diverse groups, it may be helpful to develop relations among teachers and community ethnic organizations. As teachers interact with these community ethnic organizations, they will begin to recognize their own cultural beingness, and the community ethnic organizations will reap the benefit of having their own cultures validated. This provides a valuable bonding for teachers that will serve them well at Level Two.

By the end of Level One, there will be the beginnings of a

relatively safe environment in which teachers begin to explore the nature of culture, as it manifests itself in themselves, and begin to recognize and acknowledge their ignorance and ethnocentrism about other cultures.

As stated earlier, Level Two manifests both process and product. Following the ICW format, we find at this level a great deal of self-awareness being developed. The culture bump methodology serves this function very well. After having examined the nature of culture, ethnocentrism and communication (or lack of it) within the relatively low-risk area of simulation ethnic or cultural activities, the participants are now ready to examine their ignorance and prejudice about various ethnic groups within the United States. In fact, the first ethnic group that they study is their own. At this time, we can also see the three skills defined by Geneva Gay being developed. The culture bump methodology provides the structure for the teacher candidates to examine their own cultural expectations of teachers and students in the classroom—based on actual experience. This removes those expectations from the realm of normal behavior and places them in the arena of cultural reactions, thus giving the teacher the objectivity needed to redesign his or her teaching style and techniques to reach all the children in a classroom.

It is also at this level that culture specific information, or single group studies focused on specific groups—Chinese American, Italian American, Mexican American—should be introduced. While the individual reflection process continues, the teacher learns how to assess racist, sexist, and elitist overtones in textbooks and other materials while doing in-depth study of various ethnic groups including one's own. Teachers having been trained in using the culture bump, will be able to learn about differences in others without having those differences reinforce stereotypes. This begins to prepare students to fulfill James Banks' (1973) goal to

> ...develop the ability to make reflective decisions so that they can resolve personal problems, and through social

action, influence public policy and develop a sense of political efficacy. (p. 152)

By Level Three, with its process innovations from Level Two and philosophical orientation, we find little need for cross-cultural methodology since the goal to create an environment in which teachers and students are empowered to create their own learning situations has been reached. At this level, we find a curriculum in which an approach for education that is multicultural and social reconstructionist is spontaneously occurring. Upon reaching this level, teachers and students have been given the tools to continuously identify and rectify their own cultural blind spots and can, as a group and as individuals, uncover their own strengths.

Results:
Integration of Cross-Cultural Communication and Typology of Multicultural Curriculum

Let us look at results of a systematic integration of cross-cultural communication methods into a multicultural curriculum. A neutral or safe environment would be created in which teachers and students can examine honestly their own ethnocentrism, racism, and prejudices—always within the context of moving beyond these self-damaging and other-damaging attitudes and beliefs. There would be a focus on developing the skill of communicating—in all its implications—with people who are different.

A vision of an America in which perfect multiculturalism existed—an America in which cultural diversity is respected, ethnocentric and prejudicial attitudes have been overcome, degrading poverty and dehumanizing dependency have been eradicated, and all people have developed a meaningful identity—would become the shared vision that guides the newly prepared teachers. With the discovery of their group and individual vision, participants are ready to be educators for the children of this new society.

How Does One Respond When Teachers Question Whether Multicultural Inclusiveness Is Consistent with What Is Valued in America?

The institutional and professional leadership should help teachers understand that multicultural education is verbally incorporated into the major documents upon which this country was founded: *The Constitution of the United States*, the *Declaration of Independence*, the *Bill of Rights*, and other major documents broadly embraced. The difficulty is that our school and other practices have not included all Americans. That is why America has had to amend some of these documents to grant citizenship and the right to vote to many not originally included by traditional practices.

We must help all teachers comprehend that the ideas of pluralizing the curriculum are not inconsistent with what America stands for in either values or behaviors. In fact, it is the reform movement of our time to assist the country in aligning its practices with what was proposed in the very documents which we have always embraced.

Some Essential Aspects of Program Execution (Re: Multicultural Transformation)

Earlier, we discussed the introduction and the perspective that will be needed for effective upgrading of the school's program. Following are six essential aspects of the total program execution.

1. Commitment

There must be commitment to the objectives of an upgraded multicultural curriculum experience and what it can do for today's learners. There must be commitment to the general tenets of equity, to preserving the dignity of every learner, and to the constructs of democratic living. Such commitment causes one to direct all professional efforts toward this outcome. Further, there must be commitment to the *Constitution of the United States*, to the *Bill of Rights* (including the rights of all academic consumers), and to the *Declaration of Independence*. These are followed by commitment to the academic enterprise in one's local community. Finally, there must be commitment to a society which is open, diverse, nonviolent, and supportive of all its inhabitants.

2. Consciousness

Educators must be individually conscious of inconsistencies that exist in American institutions and some families. Few problems can be resolved until those with the authority to solve them are conscious that a problem exists. Building the consciousness is a necessary step for those providing leadership for such curriculum upgrading. There must also be a functional consciousness of inequity in school programming, of instructional behavior, of poverty and its implications, of practices of exclusion. Finally, there must be consciousness of patterns of victimization. Over a period of time, if practices, procedures, and decisions have reduced the chances of any client or student to benefit maximally from programming, this constitutes victimization.

3. Cohesiveness

There must be a cohesiveness of learning experiences reflected in the planning, execution, and evaluation of curriculum activity. Multicultural upgrading is not a disjointed set of experiences which can be imported or exported at will, for it involves a process embracing the best that we know about learning, teaching, curriculum implementation, human intellectual functioning, and social growth. This cohesiveness also involves a congruency with instruction needed for general cognitive skill acquisition.

4. Collaboration

Multicultural curriculum transformation requires that those involved connect with others in confronting change. We emphasize the need for confrontations that are "friendly" in style, framework, and approach. One must definitely collaborate with new levels of ethnic literacy and with new frameworks for interacting with difference.

5. Competence

There must be the development of competence in cross-racial, cross-ethnic literacy. This competence in human service delivery in diverse settings must include comprehension of the dynamics of instruction. This level of competence embraces administrative functioning as well, including policy setting, procedure establishment, and program monitoring.

6. Courage

Of all the foregoing essentials, this one is the most critical because leadership for change is also an emotional experience. One must have the courage to believe he or she can make a difference. Then one must act on that belief on behalf of America's children within the academic arena as well as the larger society. A key element of courage capacity is the ability to accept criticism and the objections that come from those who oppose as well as those who are at different stages of their understanding. Finally, there must be courage to counteract all who say that schools (and thus the curriculum) have no place in the task of transforming America.

For Further Thought

1. Why is it significant for educators to internalize the concept of multiculturalism at Baptiste's typological levels II and III? Identify two distinctive characteristics of each level.

2. Design a strategy for teaching a concept or topic that will reflect level II of Baptiste's typology. How could you move this strategy to level III?

3. Describe a cultural bump that may have happened to you or someone you know. Identify several cultural bump situations that may occur in an educational setting.

4. Describe intercultural communication. What is meant by this concept?

5. Many educators consider commitment to be the most essential of the Essential Aspects of program execution. What is commitment? Do you agree that this is the most essential? Why or why not?

6. What are some of the difficulties of collaboration? Give three examples of collaboration.

References Cited

Archer, C. (1990). *Living with strangers in the USA*. Englewood Cliffs, NJ: Prentice Hall.

Banks, J.A., (Ed.). (1973). *Teaching ethnic studies*. Washington, DC: National Council for the Social Studies.

Baptiste, Jr., H.P. (1983). Internalizing the concept of multiculturalism. In Samucla, R.O. & Woods, S.L. (Eds.), *Perspectives in Immigrant and Minority Education*. Washington, DC: University Press of America, 294-308.

Baptiste, Jr., H.P. (1994). The multicultural environment of schools. Implications to leaders. In Hughes, L. (Ed.), *The Principal as Leader*. New York: Merrill/MacMillan, 89-109.

Baptiste, Jr., H.P. & Archer, C. (1994). A comprehensive multicultural teacher education program: An idea whose time has come. In Atwater, M., *et al.* (Eds.), *Multicultural education: Inclusion of all*. Athens, GA: University of Georgia, 65-90.

Baptiste, M.L. & Baptiste, Jr., H.P. (1980). *Competencies toward multicultrualism or Multicultural teacher education: Preparing educators to provide educational equity*, Vol. 1. Washington, DC: American Association of Colleges for Teacher Education.

Barna, L.M. & Jain, N.C. (1978). Teaching of intercultural communication at the undergraduate and graduate levels. In Hoopes, D.S., Pedersen, P.B. & Renwick, G.W. (Eds.), *Overview of intercultural education, training and research*, Vol. 2, *Education and training*. Washington, DC: Society for Intercultural Education, Training, and Research.

Brislin, R.W. (1981). *Cross-cultural encounters: Face-to-face interaction*. Elmsford, NY: Pergamon.

Brislin, R., Cushner, K., Cherries, C., & M. Yong. (1976). *Beyond culture*. New York: Anchor Press.

Brislin, R., Cushner, K., Cherries, C., & M. Yong. (1986). *Intercultural interactions: A practical guide*. Beverly Hills, CA: Sage.

Hoopes, D.S., & Ventura, P. (1979). *Intercultural sourcebook*. LaGrange Park, IL: Intercultural Network.

Pusch, M.D., (Ed.) (1979). *Multicultural education: A cross cultural training approach*. Chicago, IL: Intercultural Press.

Shirts, R.G. (1973). "Bafa Bafa" Simile II. Post Office Box 910, Delman, CA, 92014.

Sleeter, C.E. & Grant, C.A. (1987). An analysis of multicultural education in the United States. *Harvard Educational Review*, 57 (4), 421-439.

Stewart, E.C. (1971). *American cultural patterns: A cross-cultural perspective*. Chicago, IL: Intercultural Press.

Stewart, E.C. (1973). Dimensions in cross cultural instruction. Paper presented at the International Communication Convention, April.

Suzuki, B.H. (1984). Curriculum transformation for multicultural education. *Education and Urban Society*, 11, 294-322.

Notes

All knowledge
comes from
socially diverse
roots.

—H. Prentice
Baptiste, Jr.

Chapter 7

Moving
the Environment
toward Multiculturalism

Embracing Multicultural Thinking

Educators in this decade will help in their own development for the tasks which lie ahead by asking themselves the following question:

In the provision of educational services to academic consumers, how can I check my perceptions of clients who are culturally different from the teacher, or other service provider?

Also, one might ask:

What is my role in the elimination of illiteracy in America's workforce?

How can I enhance appreciation of diversity in the curriculum? In the school-at-large, and in its procedures, activities, and guidance program?

What Are the Components of a Multicultural School Environment?

The Nebraska Department of Education

The Nebraska Department of Education (1993) listed the following in describing their recommended environment:

1. The contributions of men and women of various ethnic and cultural groups integrated across the curriculum from preschool through 12th grade and beyond.

2. Teaching by modifying the instruction in ways that facilitate students' learning styles and abilities.

3. Readily available resource materials in the media center that provide current and unbiased information about the African American, the Hispanic American, the Native American, and the Asian American.

4. Diversity reflected in the assembly programs, the decorations, school lunch menus, and other general areas.

5. Encouraging all students to participate in school activities and extra curricular events.

6. A staff that reflects diversity of race, ethnicity, and gender.

Official Endorsement of Multicultural Transformation

Another essential element will be the endorsement of curriculum upgrading by persons in official positions with school programs (school boards, curriculum councils, staff development centers, service centers, curriculum advisory groups, and others). Keeping such groups informed is a beginning step.

While it will be essential to keep them informed, it may also be necessary to help them understand the parameters of multicultural understandings and why such upgrading is desirable for today's learners at all levels.

Creation of a Policy on Diversity in Curriculum

It is recommended that an official policy on curriculum upgrading for diversity be established. Most new policy declarations require sophisticated political skills by those supporting such action. We suggest that a clearly stated policy be created and submitted to any policy-making body. Such endorsement enhances the execution of program upgrading.

In the State of Nebraska, much action began when a state legislator introduced legislation which would impact the curriculum of every school in the State. Much work is underway to assist school districts understand the curriculum action—particularly where culturally different students are not enrolled in a given school. When a policy is established, one should work to be sure that its dissemination is as comprehensive as possible.

Suggestions for Curriculum Leadership

What might be the focus of curriculum activity in the various stages of the transformations? Following is a listing of suggestions for what might be undertaken in the way of curriculum activity, whether it is through various committees, commissions, or large group activity:

1. Understanding Multicultural Curriculum Development

Develop an understanding of curriculum development undertaken from a multicultural perspective.

2. Accepting the Tenets of Multicultural Curriculum

Assure equity and social justice, and eliminate curriculum bias and instructional discrimination.

3. Increasing Ethnic and Linguistic Literacy

Discover the research on how second language learning occurs—and learn more about culturally different people.

4. Analyzing Societal Institutions

In what ways, for example, are museums and galleries embracing diversity? Are textbook companies upgrading their publications?

5. Recognizing Poverty and Learning Relationships

Undertake specific curriculum study of program components which address how impoverished learners approach the schooling experience. Perspective and perception are key elements of all learning. While we have had "poverty programs" for some time, little research and curriculum study have been devoted to learning.

6. Understanding National Programs, Resolutions, and Mandates

Part of the institutionalization of multicultural upgrading is the "official" endorsements and "semi-official" embracing by recognized literacy or curriculum bodies. Some curriculum activity could be devoted to exploring national societies (The Association for Supervision and Curriculum Development, the National Association for Multicultural Education, the International Reading Association, the National Council of Teachers of English, the National Association for Bilingual Education, the National Council of Teachers of Mathematics, the National Science Teachers Association, etc.) and their work related to multicultural upgrading within disciplines and among disciplines.

7. Examining Stereotypes and Images

This could be an interesting beginning activity to help school programs examine the existing stereotypes about people in and out of the school community.

8. Activitating Demonstration Lessons

Often, there are creative teachers within a school or school district who could share "demonstration lessons" with colleagues on how to integrate ethnic content into lessons, units, or segments. Also, literature teachers, for example, may demonstrate how ethnically diverse literary selections may be used to reach the same cognitive objectives already established for certain aspects of the program of studies.

9. Analyzing Library Holdings

While most librarians are keenly aware of their acquisitions and holdings, it might be helpful to have a group of teachers, parents, and community people explore libraries for various kinds of materials related to culturally different persons or groups. They should then share their assessments with librarians and others in a collaborative effort at upgrading. Some might suggest that such acquisitions are not needed if culturally different learners are not enrolled. Our position is that such materials are needed even more urgently if learners do not have daily exposure to diversity through school mates and instructional staff members.

10. Employing Current Content
(Especially Newspapers)

Ethnic newspapers are a rich source of current data on culturally different populations. Their use by teachers is urged.

11. Reviewing the Testing Program

This involves reviewing the assessment philosophy of a given school or school district. Explorations should be made of standardized tests, teacher-made tests, and other factors including the teaching of test-taking skills. (This is offered on the assumption that, philosophically, educators want all learners to learn, to succeed, and to have a positive schooling experience under their guidance).

12. Reviewing the Student Activities Program
(Co-Curricular Activities)

Which student activities are unbalanced in terms of diversity? What kinds of influences are active in the choice of student activities? In a school where racial and ethnic diversity exists, what kind of efforts are made at inclusiveness?

13. Examining School Food Services

What messages are delivered as a result of the menus planned for school consumption? Which cultures are represented? Why? What is the relationship between what is planned and what some groups consider adequate nutritional intake?

14. Assessing School Social Services

A major element of this involves the issue of cross-racial, cross-ethnic social service. Also, does the school social service effort provide an understanding of cultural factors in service provision?

15. Conducting a Curriculum Analysis

This could involve how a faculty uses direct instructional time and on which topics, groups, or issues. While America has no national curriculum, the administration of national tests for assessment continues. Part of the curriculum analysis would explore which ethnic, racial, and linguistic groups are empha-sized in the curriculum, as reflected by the amount of time spent on any given group.

These fifteen points represent beginning efforts at curricu-lum study toward the goal of multicultural upgrading. Organiz-ing for curriculum study requires the skill of group leadership. Which persons can best influence the thinking of others? How is this used to best advantage on behalf of multicultural curricu-lum upgrading?

The Cognitive, Affective and Psychomotor Domains

Issues of multicultural curriculum transformation will nec-essarily involve the cognitive domain, the affective domain, and the psychomotor domain because each is necessary and consis-tent with diversity. How people feel about their experiences is one of the critical points of curriculum leadership. With learners who are children, we must constantly explore and monitor their emotional reaction to multicultural learnings. The academic socialization of teachers and other curriculum workers will constitute the determining factor on how well learners embrace diversity in the classroom.

Cognitive

Visual stimulation is important. What does one see as one undertakes the learning tasks? What messages are delivered?

Affective

How sincere is the instructional interaction? To what extent does the school embrace the presence of diversity within the curriculum?

Psychomotor

The psychomotor domain will allow for diverse channels through which alternative learning styles can be addressed. This is a very important dimension of the learning processes of young children. In some cultures this domain is very significant in the acquiring of knowledge.

Because so much of the school curriculum is framed within the cognitive domain, most practitioners will have a more thorough comprehension of cognitive processes. We do, however, embrace Howard Gardner's (1983) concepts of multiple intelligences and the recognition of such within the multicultural transformation of America's curriculum.

For Further Thought

1. What do you think are the major components of a multicultural classroom environment? Will these components differ for the school's environment? Why or why not?

2. How does one transform a curriculum?

3. Why is it helpful to have a policy on diversity in the curriculum? What does it mean to have a policymaking board refuse to adopt such a policy?

4. Choose any one of the "suggestions for leadership" and outline steps which should be undertaken to enhance that area of curriculum development for multicultural transformation. Please identify a minimum of five such steps and describe each step. Then cite why you consider these steps appropriate and useful.

References Cited

Gardner, H. (1983). *Frames of mind*. New York: Basic Books.

Nebraska Department of Education. (1993). Rule 16 Approval of school district multicultural education programs. Lincoln, NE: Equal Education Opportunities Section (301 Centennial Mall South, Lincoln, NE 68509).

Other References

DeVilla, R.A., Faltis, C.J., & Cummins, J.P. (Eds.). (1994). *Cultural diversity in schools*. Albany, NY: State University of New York Press.

Diaz-Rico, L. & Weed, K.Z. (1995). *Crosscultural language and academic development handbook*. Boston, MA: Allyn & Bacon.

Gonzales, J., Roberts, H., Harris, O.D., Huff, D.J., Johns, A.M., Ray. L., & Scott, O.L. (1994). *Teaching from a multicultural perspective*. Thousand Oaks, CA: Sage.

Hollins, E.R., King, J.E., & Hayman, W.C. (1994). *Teaching diverse populations*. Albany, NY: State Univeristy of New York Press.

Jordan C., Tharp, R.G., & Baird-Vogt, L. (1992). Chapter 1. In Saravior-Shon, M. & Arvizu, S. (Eds.). *Cross-cultural literacy: Ethnographies of communication in multiethnic classrooms*. New York: Garland.

Kanpol, B. & McLaren, P. (Eds.). (1995). *Critical multiculturalism: Uncommon voices in a common struggle*. Westport, CT: Bergin & Garvey.

Lynch, E.W. & Hanson, M.J. (1992). *Developing cultural competence*. Baltimore, MD: Paul H. Brookes.

Pignatelli, F. & Pflaum, S.W. (1993). *Celebrating diverse voices*. Newbury Park, CA: Corwin Press.

Robinson, B.J. & Shade, C. (Eds.). (1989). *Culture, style, and the educative process*. Springfield, IL: Charles C. Thomas.

Spindler, G. & Spindler, L. (Eds.). (1994). *Pathways to cultural awareness*. Thousand Oaks, CA: Corwin Press.

...I believe racism
has killed more
people than speed,
heroin, or cancer,
and will continue to kill
until it is no more.

—Alice Childress

Chapter 8

Cross-Racial, Cross-Ethnic Teaching and Learning

The Dynamics of Instruction

Instructional dynamics involve all of the elements operative whenever one or more persons attempts to provide instruction for others. A "dynamic" is an evolving entity which emerges under the context of communication in a helping relationship. Above anything else, instruction is an act of communication by a person more experienced with the content, skills, and concepts to be learned than is the person(s) in the role of learner.

Historically, instruction has been perceived as consisting primarily of verbal language intended to increase cognition. Today, it is understood that it is much more than that—and whenever the parties (teacher and learners) are uniquely different from each other, additional dynamics come into action.

Cross-Racial, Cross-Ethnic Instruction

Whenever the teacher represents one racial or ethnic identity and the learner represents another identity during an episode of pedagogy, there is cross-racial, cross-ethnic instruction. The racial or ethnic history of the teacher and the learner will dictate the degree of apprehension, concern, and distortion which may enter such instructional relationship.

Historically, this category of helping relationships have been under-emphasized both in teacher preparation in and in the execution of teaching responsibilities. Race and ethnic relations emerge as either positive or negative (as a result of the history of race relations in America) and they consistently impact the pedagogical experience.

The History of Race-Ethnic Relations in America

In the United States, race and ethnic relations have been framed in the legal elements of a model of a superior-inferior mode. School desegregation sought to dismantle a system which defined, structurally supported, and enhanced such a model based on race. Because so many of the regions of the United States practiced school segregation, programs which prepared teachers did not emphasize cross-racial human service. Students and teachers who were racially alike participated in instructional settings in which cultural understandings were considered a low priority because so much was understood about each other. No cultural questions needed to be asked because the teacher's background and the learner's background were so similar. Learning styles and teaching styles were so well known that little energy went into the research of such entities.

Today, thousands of classrooms are engaged in cross-racial, cross-ethnic teaching and learning. The dynamics of such settings are not well understood at this point and few teacher education programs are researching and/or addressing such issues. This is true despite the fact that more than ninety percent of the new teachers entering teaching represent the profile of Caucasian, English-speaking, middle-class, suburban or rural backgrounds, while more and more learners (especially in the twenty-five largest cities of the United States) are culturally different from their teachers' profiles.

Why Does This Make a Difference?

At an earlier time, many people thought that race and ethnicity made no difference in the instructional process. This was when instruction was thought to be a one-way street, and the learners were to remain essentially "passive" in the process. Today, communication specialists, curriculum planners, instructional researchers, and a host of other specialists concerned with instructional interaction are now discussing and explaining the dynamics of cross-racial, cross-ethnic pedagogy.

The Psychology of Cross-Racial Instruction

The instructional assumption of cognitive growth through the sense of hearing (as the primary learning channel) has not resulted in the level of achievement desired by many nor the commitment to nonviolence needed for these times. Remembering that instruction is a major experience in communication, the psychological reference embraces how people feel about the instructional act or its appropriateness. It also embraces how the teacher feels about those being instructed. How one feels includes one's racial history especially, as it sends a message regarding adequacy of one's existence as a human being. The instructor's feeling about those being instructed is matched on the other side of the desk by the way the learner feels about the teacher.

This emphasis, however, is on the professional responsibility for serving public education as it attempts to upgrade itself through a multicultural restructuring. Growing out of the teacher's own racial history (especially in the first eighteen years of the teacher's life), there is a set of concerns which one must address:

1. Are these learners worthy of being taught?

2. How important does this set of learners appear to be to the future of America?

3. Does the instructor feel that the learners were adequately responsive to that particular segment of instruction? If so, why? If not, why?

4. Instructional preference for specific learners carries a strong expectation that the instruction will have a high level of affective receptivity by learners.

Such psychological dynamics are an ingredient of building an instructional relationship with learners.

Race, however, is such a powerful variable that one must analyze the prevailing assumptions of Caucasian normalcy and any culturally-different abnormality as perceived by many in the larger society. America is still struggling with the notion of white supremacy and neither the curriculum nor the teacher preparation institutions have adequately addressed these with prospective teachers. One cannot ignore the constant efforts of traditional social scientists in attempting to document the "deficits" of culturally different people—especially African Americans. These realities, coupled with the daily experiences of many culturally different persons regarding race relations, leave many students with limited trust in any cross-racial helping relationship.

Cross-racial instruction, then, cannot ignore the fact that the curriculum adopted for America's schools was devoid of a curricular validation for the culturally-different. In many instances, the culturally-different learner was pejoratively defined—as a problem. People of color were often assaulted in curriculum materials required for school use. At other times, people of color were invisible in the academic institution at any respectable level. Being normal was equivalent to being Caucasian, English-speaking, and middle income. Messages of "duplication" were forceful and difference was rejected.

What Are Some Prescriptions for Cross-Racial, Cross-Ethnic Teaching?

First, one has to reconceptualize the professional framework of instruction. How do we see the art and science of instruction? What has been our prevailing view of race and ethnic relations? Parker Palmer (1990) notes that good teaching comes from the identity and integrity of the teacher. The act of teaching is an intersection between the "public person and the private person." In some ways, this can be a dangerous intersection, but nowhere can justice be more adequately demonstrated than during the instructional act.

Palmer further states that all cannot be reduced to technique. Such effort can trivialize what can become a beautiful instructional interchange. Persons offering their services in cross-racial, cross-ethnic settings should return to a major analysis of their instructional philosophy.

A second prescription for cross-racial, cross-ethnic teaching is the deliberate attempt to move—from control as an emphasis in teaching to the construction of hope within students. America no longer needs a "power-based" instructional performance. Effective teachers need to engage in classroom "power sharing." Power sharing leads to empowerment of the learners. Discover ways through which learners can engage in more decision-making within curriculum and instructional matters.

A third prescription is the building of an instructional relationship across the racial-ethnic lines. What is an instructional relationship?

> An instructional relationship occurs when learner and teacher are able to comfortably connect with each other within a context of being, belonging, or working together. It further includes the teaching-learning attitude which two or more persons assume toward one

another. Such element includes the state of being mutually or reciprocally interested in the same enterprise (learning). The development of an instructional relationship across racial lines or across ethnic lines...will rest, in part, on the psychological health of both the teacher and learner. It is understood that this relationship takes into account the racial history and/or ethnic history of each participant. This relationship requires that the two or more parties engage in behaviors which will be perceived to be mutually desirable and beneficial to all participants. Although our focus is on cross-racial, cross-ethnic instructional settings, this same principle applies in cross-gender instruction as gender is an issue in the complexity of all relationships. Race and gender are such powerful variables that all relationships are conditioned thereby.

NOTE: Cross-gender teaching is treated in Chapter 13.

Instructional Discrimination

Another prescription for cross-racial, cross-ethnic teaching is the deliberate attention to the prevention of instructional discrimination. Instructional discrimination is the pedagogical act, practice, or behavior that results in unfair or inappropriate response to the varied or culturally-influenced learning styles of students being served. Further, it is any assumption that all persons learn best from listening to the teacher. Equal instructional opportunity or equal learning opportunity results when varied teaching approaches are employed so that varied learning styles may receive an appropriate reaction or response.

We make the assumption that no serious teacher would knowingly discriminate instructionally across racial lines.

The Principle of Distributive Justice
(Re: Cross-Racial, Cross-Ethnic Teaching)

When short-changed participants develop the emotion of anger and act to break off a disadvantageous exchange, the principle of distributive justice is operative. No episode of anger is intended to last very long. If and when it does, it creates a major imbalance in any relationship, especially an instructionally-helping relationship.

If either the teacher or the learner feels short-changed in the exchange, anger—both expressed anger and non-expressed anger—can negatively impact the intended outcomes of instruction and learning.

Instructional Behavior
Which Seeks Student Empowerment

Empowerment involves the freedom to define one's own self, one's role, and one's ethnic racial identity—and to share that with others from a framework of an equitable academic and social environment. It embraces the permission to celebrate one's life, one's self, and one's contributions through a life-affirming channel. Lives and existences are valued in environments which empower clients.

If clients feel powerless and with no opportunity for empowerment, they conclude that their lives are not valued. Any time one's own life is not valued, then the lives of those around him or her are also not valued.

Cross-racial, cross-ethnic instruction must seek to empower learners at a level even higher than in same-race, same-ethnic group settings because of the history of race and ethnic relations in America. Empowerment involves issues of comparable human worth, ethnic literacy, life experiences, economic diversity, gender, and visibility. It also involves understanding various elements of the dynamics of instruction.

For Further Thought

1. Explain cross-racial and cross-ethnic teaching and cite several examples of its occurence in an instructional setting.

2. Why are the dynamics of a cross-cultural or cross-ethnic setting so important to understand? Identify three to five dynamics that may emerge from the cross-cultural nature of a classroom and/or school.

3. Describe several strategies, settings, or educational approaches that would be empowering to the participating students.

Reference Cited

Palmer, P. (1990). The Courage to Teach and to Learn. A speech given as part of the Chester E. Peters Lecture and Student Development Series, Kansas State University, Manhattan, KS, November 29.

Notes

Lifetime
perspectives
are never void
of curriculum
content and
instructional
relationships.

—James B. Boyer

Chapter 9

Critical Issues for Practitioners

Theoreticians and philosophers have roles which do not always allow them to operationalize theories, philosophies, or beliefs. On the other hand, the practitioner—those involved daily in teaching, learning, administering, counseling, and identifying curriculum resources—must transform an idea, a theory, or a concept into practice with learners and others whose lives are intimately involved with schooling.

Once the practitioner embraces that responsibility, he or she must allow oneself to begin the process of conceptualizing the framework within which such curriculum operations must occur. Additionally, there are issues associated with operationalizing the curriculum which might be helpful to those charged with "making schools work" for all learners.

Critical Issue 1:
The Teaching Credential or Certificate

Most states in the United States issue certificates that are a declaration that the holder has at least minimum professional preparation for an instructional or other role with learners under the age of eighteen. In America, the protection of children in all facets of life is still a priority. We are happy that no state has rejected that responsibility. This is why most states have programs of child protection services available to all its citizens.

The teaching certificate is, in an academic way, part of the child protection process. The holder is expected to be able to function in an instructional (or related) role on behalf of children. Presently, no state requires that postsecondary educators declare their preparation through a state-issued credential. Thus, the protection of children, the instruction of children, and the safety of children all remain part of the basic reasons that we are asked to hold a certificate.

The certificate, however, implies that one can teach any child or learner who arrives at the schoolhouse door for instructional services. Any child means a child of any race, gender, language, exceptionality, perspective, culture, or experience. Given this, the practitioner must begin to re-evaluate the meaning of the certificate.

The following carries that responsibility to its affective instructional level:

> As a teacher, my job is to connect up with whoever shows
> up Monday morning.
>
> —Ethel Hixson

The instructional practitioner, then, must ask how he or she can deliver this level of service if they know so little about learners different from oneself? This concern will require that both preservice teacher education—as well as staff development for those already engaged in full-time instructional services— enter a program or process of increasing ethnic literacy, especially about learners unlike themselves.

Our certificates say that we can teach anything to any child who enters our classroom or learning center. In implementing a multicultural educational program, the instructional responsibility then moves to yet a higher level which is embraced by the following:

> You can't teach a child whom you do not KNOW
> You can't come back if you never go
> You can't be a leader if no one follows you
> You can't be a teacher if no one BELIEVES in you.
> —James B. Boyer

Certificates do not declare that learners believe in you. They merely imply that you have been exposed to specific kinds of instruction prior to the acquisition of the certificate. The real teacher is one who has a certificate and has the demonstrated skills of serving all children. Those who would lead America in its transformation must spend time on the meaning of academic credentials and the level of accountability now required for a multicultural curriculum to be effective.

Critical Issue 2: How Can We Help Educators and Others Who Do Not Understand the Urgency of Multicultural Transformation of the Curriculum?

One must use the energy and force of one's own personality, one's instructional expertise, and one's most sophisticated level of persuasive skills to reach some persons who do not yet understand why multicultural concerns are so urgent. Many of those persons are actually well-meaning individuals whose "habits of analysis" lead them to raise questions of legitimacy. This is to be expected. The initial understanding must include a knowledge that some of these are the same voices who said that desegregation would never be a reality in America. They also said that the women's equity movement would never surface at any meaningful level. They could not envision that more and more women would seek and hold public office as governors, mayors, commissioners, senators, representatives, school superintendents, pastors, bishops, or other roles traditionally held by men. So one must realize that while they have felt that the ultimate transformation of the curriculum would be detrimental to America's goals, they must now be convinced that the absence of multicultural curriculum will be one of the most detrimental factors America has ever experienced.

Additionally, we must help them understand that:

Multicultural education is not ethnic cheerleading or gender cheerleading;

It is not just a "feel good" curriculum concerned only with aspects of the affective domain of learning;

It is not devoid of academic rigor and scholarly production skills—although it does expand the concept of scholarly production skills; and

It is not an esoteric topic for a few people in a given school setting.

What, then, is multicultural curriculum? First, it is a curriculum of inclusion which attempts to involve people of color, appropriate images, and the roles and contributions of women as well as men to our society. The concepts of equity and diversity are presented as strengths rather than as detriments. It is not a lowering of academic quality, or the destruction of the "united" concept of the United States.

Secondly, multicultural curriculum is pedagogically sound in that it promotes culturally-responsive instruction. Historically, the American school has assumed that all learners learn the same way, on the same day, in the same amount of time. This fallacy has resulted in the alienation of many learners of all races, colors, creeds, genders, and languages. Multicultural curriculum calls for a cultural sensitivity that respects the learning styles of children and requests that instruction upgrade itself to meet more than one style. Such pedagogical responsibility includes the arrangement of classrooms or learning centers, the need for learners to spend more time in "action centers" or in active roles rather than passive listening, and increased or alternative channels through which assessment of learning may be conducted (evaluation).

Multicultural curriculum is a curriculum of excellence and sophistication in diverse thinking. For years, America has talked about excellence in education. Our position is that you cannot have excellence without equity. You can never have an excellent curriculum which is monocultural, if America is truly multicultural in its population makeup. There are those who believe that one can have an excellent curriculum which is also exclusive, sexist, racist, and without a social justice agenda. Sophisticated practitioners know better. They know that America cannot afford to write off this growing segment of knowledge, understanding, and skill development. The school curriculum can only be excellent when it prepares learners to function in a multicultural society.

Earlier curriculum efforts—including the many curriculum reform movements—implied that issues of race, economic class, gender, or language were insignificant. Except for disaggregated test scores, little effort was made to consider the positive elements of difference. We now know that multicultural education demands that the content of curriculum must be inclusive of people of color, inclusive of issues that affect people's lives, and reflective of the new concerns of a society faced with the problems of the coming century. In a society that depends on the curriculum of the schools to guard the intellect of America, such guardianship must be characterized by an inclusive curriculum effort. Multicultural education is that banner of inclusiveness.

Multicultural education is scholarly and has an ample research base (Banks & Banks, 1995). The traditional academic community—including many of the more than three million teachers in America—tends to question the scholarly base of multicultural concerns in the curriculum. This is to be expected, because intellectual styles always call for evidence of scholarship in their examination of new forums. While the study of specific ethnic groups was undertaken as much as sixty years ago by some social scientists, multicultural education is a relatively new field of study which emerged within the last three decades. Most of the books, research studies, and creative endeavors in the academic community are dated since 1970. This would suggest that while multicultural education is yet a new field of study, it emerged when America was moving to an information society and scores of researchers, writers, curriculum specialists, and others engaged in the production of scholarly works embracing Ethnic Studies, Black Studies, Chicano Studies, Women's Studies, Native American Studies, and scores of others. Centers like the Japanese American Curriculum Project, and the Centers for Urban Education and Centers for Multicultural Education all emerged during a time when America was questioning its move to a more equitable society.

Yes, multicultural education is scholarly based. As with any academic movement, the critics will be vocal and descriptive. However, the scholarship efforts will continue. The authors of this handbook were both founding members of the National Association for Multicultural Education, which holds an annual conference each year and is growing in membership both nationally and internationally.

Critical Issue 3:
What Are Some of the Real Agenda Items for the Curriculum of the School in a Multicultural Society?

No curriculum, as we've stated, can be considered functional in the year 2000 which does not have a major social justice agenda. As America lives with limited skills of intergroup relations, poorer skills of race and ethnic relations, and few instructional skills of cross-racial, cross-ethnic teaching, the curriculum must embrace an agenda of social justice. What good does it do for one American to master the content and information of whatever is being taught if the rage, hatred, and exclusion of Americans unlike one's self is so strong that no one appreciates the other?

This social justice agenda includes visions of a society where all human beings are perceived as equal entities. It includes a recognition of the value of all lives being worthy of preservation. It includes the understanding that the dignity of all human beings—including children of color and children who are exceptional and/or physically challenged—must be preserved in classrooms, study halls, athletic activities, music activities, and scores of other places.

The multicultural curriculum agenda requires that learners engage not just what **are**—but what they **mean**. This forces instruction to consider issues of exploitation, oppression, scarcity, and diversity. This certainly includes different perspectives on the same event. (Example: In teaching American history to children, what is really meant by the Westward movement? Was it the Westward movement for Asians whose ancestors might have entered the continental United States through Seattle or San Francisco?)

Multicultural curriculum seeks to have learners develop a social consciousness as well as intellectual competence. The social consciousness allows the learner to act on issues, programs, legislation, and policies which may be detrimental to some Americans. It forces one to ask if the principles of the *United States Constitution*, the *Bill of Rights*, the *Declaration of Independence*, and all the major documents of our society are equally applicable to all of America's citizens. One must use these ideas as a basis for curriculum development, curriculum improvement, and instructional enhancement. Otherwise, America really can become disunited.

Multicultural education teaches the skills of diversity. Such skills include how to respect people and profiles different from one's own. It allows for a "friendly confrontation" with some traditions which were never questioned before. There is a channel for the development of a commitment to equity, a commitment so sorely needed as we enter the new century.

The need to remember a fact may not be as important as the need to entertain an idea. The school is the major institution available to change thought in America. Changing our thoughts about the value of human beings would ultimately decrease the violence—academic violence, instructional violence, etc.—now prevalent in many corners of the American academic enterprise.

Critical Issue 4:
What Are the Differences between Global Education and Multicultural Education?

Some years ago, the National Council for the Social Studies provided strong leadership for helping the curriculum begin to see our world as a "global village," one in which we would all see ourselves as interdependent with all other peoples all over the world, even in countries we view as developing countries. This was a successful venture in that it occurred around the time that telecommunications and the technology industry began their expansion. Today, the superhighway has made it possible for Americans to witness events all over the world as they unfold. Additionally, global education was designed to have learners embrace an understanding of cultures and peoples outside the United States and to comprehend how those groups impact our lives and our society. Understanding the interaction of different cultures around the world has been global education's primary purpose.

Multicultural education grew out of America's struggle with

respecting all its citizens as equals. Beginning with race as a basis for creating laws and establishing policy, the multicultural movement then embraced poverty, gender, exceptionalities, age, religion, and other factors on which discriminatory behavior was based. The quest for social justice, honesty, and shared participation in all that America had to offer became a more complex goal and entity than many had realized.

Our position on multicultural education indicates that it begins with a "domestic focus," one through which residents of the United States would create policy, programs, and procedures which are fair to all those whose lives are impacted by them. Not only must these be fair in the perception of those who make and enforce them, they must be fair in the perception of those who must abide by them. When it comes to the school curriculum, multicultural reform attempts to move American education from a monocultural, Western civilization, English-speaking, Eurocentric, Anglo perspective to a multiculturally diverse mentality, framework, and foundation. It is designed to endorse the identification and accommodation of culturally-different people and to promote the recognition of their contributions. It is a people-oriented and relationships-oriented study which confronts patterns of thought, beliefs, and belief systems that impede the attainment of a more equitable America. Further, it attempts to reflect the totality of America's population.

Because multicultural education attempts to prepare learners to live more harmoniously with persons different from oneself, it becomes equally as important for students enrolled in programs where there is little cultural-ethnic-racial-linguistic difference among the bulk of learners enrolled. In fact, those learners who do not have a daily experience with persons of color, with persons whose first language is something other than English, with persons who come from a different economic class than they are in greater need of a curriculum which prepares them for life amid such diversity.

Hughes (1990) cites the need for such academic experience for that population:

If one is to "participate intellectually and responsibly in the pluralistic society that surrounds us, rather than in a mythical and sheltered subculture not truly representative of our nation as a whole, then a culturally aware, or multicultural education is necessary." p. 26

Global education emerged from an interest in competition with other world powers, while multicultural education emerged from an interest in social justice within the United States of America. Global education sought to spend some of its energies comparing political ideologies and some nonhuman issues. Multicultural education sought to spend much of its energies on accommodating difference when many thought that difference was detrimental to our "united" state of being. As long as difference was perceived as a negative force, educators could deny the strength which difference brought to the environments—both human and nonhuman environments.

Diversity is the basis of a strong curriculum program as well as a strong school. It is difficult for persons whose careers have kept them in monocultural environments to understand how critical it is to make the distinction between global education and multicultural education. Many such educators still see multicultural education as inappropriate for learners in settings where racial-ethnic-linguistic diversity does not exist among the learners or the professional staff. But knowing about and understanding diversity is now essential for all persons engaged in the academic or educative process. America can no longer afford to graduate persons whose exposure to difference and diversity is limited. Persons educated in such environments and with monocultural curriculum programs will be deemed incompetent for the world of the future, especially in the emerging marketplace and workplace.

What about the "Excellence" movement?

Our position is that no curriculum program can call itself excellent if it does not have diversity as its foundational base. Can any curriculum program be of high quality which systematically excludes scores of "profiles" existing in the American school today? Can any curriculum program be of high quality if it fails to provide experiences which develop cross-cultural skills?

One of the issues constantly before the American school is the extent to which learners are prepared for the entry-level workplace. Our position is that the workforce is so characterized by diversity that persons exiting the American school curriculum without some cross-cultural skill training will be at a distinct disadvantage in the competitive job market. Multicultural education's focus on humankind forces attention on the skills of human relations.

Critical Issue 5:
What Are the "Programming" Factors for a Multicultural Transformation of the Curriculum?

As part of a school or school district's effort to upgrade its curriculum for a multicultural focus, the following factors should be considered:

A. Multicultural programming for effective curriculum development requires adequate concepts of goals, objectives, and content analysis.

This involves planning and reflection on what the school's program is designed to accomplish. Goals, objectives, and program features are essential to any curriculum development effort. Because multicultural transformation involves emotional factors, it is suggested that several persons be involved in helping to define the direction of the revised goals and objectives. There must be a definite effort to make the curriculum goals more inclusive than under a monocultural focus.

This will require reviewing the existing goals and objectives for inclusive language, for the intent and content which is most reflected therein. Content analysis is one of the more complex aspects of the multicultural transformation because it forces priorities regarding which information shall be used to reach the goals and objectives. Again, in an information society, there is more information than the traditional, formal schooling process can accommodate. The goals and objectives can still be reached, but the information used to reach those goals must become more diverse. This confronts the content traditionally shared in class after class, often drawn from what one generally thinks of as the "classic curriculum" of America. Today, the upgrading of the curriculum requires some priority setting as to which information shall be used and/or emphasized.

It is well known that what learners are exposed to in formal learning settings becomes what they value, respect, and often cherish. If America is serious about remaining "united," then the content used in schools and in curriculum programming must be diverse so that it can yield a united perspective which reflects all Americans.

B. Multicultural programming demands service consciousness and population-specific conceptualization.

Those who spend their lives in the pursuit of literacy by serving in various roles in schools are part of a larger group of human service professionals. These are persons whose careers are devoted to providing service to other human beings and today those other human beings are students who represent cultural, linguistic, and racial differences from the traditional majority in America. A commitment to providing a human service to that population is critical to effective curriculum transformation.

Historically, little attention has been given to the psychological connection between teacher and learner, between counselor and client, between service provider and service consumer.

Today, multicultural curriculum reform is calling for an increased consciousness to that connection. At some point, the service provider—the educator—might need to ask if his or her service delivery is really adequate for the populations being served. This is a different focus than the traditional review to determine if a teacher can "manage" a classroom. Instead, the focus become partly self-assessment, to determine if the service provision is the most appropriate for the clients being served. How can I change or upgrade what I am doing to better meet the needs of this population?

By population-specific conceptualization, we mean the deliberate analysis of the range of learning experiences provided to learners. Does the range include content and experiences specific to the population being served? How much does one learn about people different from oneself in school? To what extent does one get academic reinforcement for the differences one brings to the curriculum experience? In other words, if a learner is Vietnamese, how much of the curriculum experience embraces the Vietnamese experience, culture, or customs? Also, much of the curricular experience will involve indirect teaching and learning. What is the magnitude of cultural difference reflected on bulletin boards? In films shown in class? In photographs used in the school? What diversity is reflected in the school's food service program?

When a program is conceptualized, a major concern for the ethnic-racial-linguistic consciousness should be included. In other words, how will the totality of this curriculum program be seen by members of the groups now considered culturally-different from the masses of learners (and teachers)?

C. Multicultural curriculum programming requires adequate program library resources for both common experiences as well as individual experiences.

It is impossible to have quality programming for learners if the instructional resources and curriculum resources are not available to implement such a program. Librarians, media specialists, and learning specialists need to collaborate on which materials will best meet the goal of diversity for learners to benefit from the program. Are the children's literature selections adequate to at least meet the resource requirements for some of the major groups representing cultural diversity (such as the Mexican American, Puerto Rican, or Native American learners in elementary schools)? Are these resources free of stereotypical reflections?

Our concern is that too little attention has been paid to the plethora of materials acquired by some school centers which may, in fact, contribute to the problem of curriculum diversity rather than to the solution of a quality program. Curriculum workers should seek to have adequacy (in quantity and quality) as a base for multicultural transformation of the materials used for curriculum and instruction.

D. Multicultural curriculum programming assumes a "process" experience which has academic justice and social justice as foundational bases.

American schooling's attention to academic justice and social justice has been limited to the "element of sameness." That is, all learners are essentially the same and democracy really means treating all learners the same, especially in our mass-produced system. Treating all learners the same implies that little analysis of instruction is necessary. Multicultural curriculum programming says that critical analysis of all instructional settings and programs is essential.

Oliver (1990), in her study of the multicultural experiences of beginning college students, raised the following kinds of concerns:

Do you recall being given either a written statement

from your secondary school or told by a school administrator or teacher that your school was committed to
providing all of the students with an education that
includes learning about the diversity of people?

If multicultural education was one of the goals of your
school, to what extent do you believe your educational
experience was influenced by this fact? Were there new
courses which reflected this change? What kinds of
student activities were planned which had this as the
main focus?

These become part of the "process" of schooling and contribute to the value of the total curriculum experience provided to
learners. Multicultural transformation is indeed as much of a
process as it is a product of the outcomes.

E. Multicultural curriculum programming should analyze learning styles of culturally-diverse populations so that instruction may have population-specific designs.

Historically, curriculum has spent little time on the cultural-
ethnic-linguistic elements of programming for schools. The body
of research on learning styles includes very little attention to
how cultural difference impacts learning styles. Multicultural
transformation calls for the deliberate exploration of the ways in
which cultural identity and ethnic-racial difference influence
the way in which a learner prefers to approach a learning task.
For example, many African American and Mexican American learners prefer to embrace learning from a cooperative
framework rather than a competitive framework. Does the
curriculum make any provisions for accommodating this learning style preference? If so, in what ways? Also, to what extent
does the curriculum actually reflect the issues of greatest con-

cern to the populations considered most "invisible" in the curriculum but who are enrolled in American schools today?

F. Multicultural curriculum programming does not deny the value of a scope-and-sequence plan, but it is still open to evolving stages of knowledge and its acquisition.

In other words, curriculum development in any framework must engage considerations of scope-and-sequence. What is the breadth of this curriculum project? How shall the experiences be organized to best meet the needs of learners? The transformation of the school curriculum does not discount the need for careful consideration given to the ordering of learning activities or to the assessment of the learning environment. Indeed, multicultural transformation calls for even greater attention to these dimensions. Of particular concern is the need for scope-and sequence which addresses the quantity of learning experiences devoted specifically to cultural difference.

Oliver (1990) addresses the scope of the curriculum experience by raising the following as part of her research on subjects immediately following secondary school:

Can you think of examples where a teacher in high school supplemented the instruction in a class by including a film focusing on cultural difference?

Or by playing music reflective of specific cultural groups?

Or by asking you to read articles or stories from publications published by or about culturally-specific groups like *Ebony* magazine or *Nuestro*?

Or by inviting a guest speaker for the class from a racial group other than your own?

Do you recall a teacher ever saying that one of the goals of a class was to further your understanding of a racial group other than your own?

Did you ever take a class than included assignments or special activities that were specifically about a racial group other than your own?

Which racial or ethnic group (other than your own) did you learn most about during your years of schooling (or your years of exposure to the curriculum)?

G. Multicultural curriculum programming must incorporate continuing evaluation for equity in interaction, content, and personnel profiles with attention to the stated objectives of the program.

To be sure, there are still persons who believe that equity and quality are incompatible as characteristics of curriculum programs. Nothing could be more fallacious. Our position is that the practitioner must professionally monitor the extent to which interaction preserves the dignity of all participants, including learners. Additionally, there must be assessment of the content being used to reach the objectives of the curriculum program. Content is to be used to reach objectives.

While some skill content may be universal in application, more than sixty percent of what is learned in school is negotiable for its exact level of essentiality. The content of the information used to teach sentence structure, for example, is imbedded in the cultural traditions of those who teach. Sentence structure can be taught even while the "indirect information" used to teach it embraces information about Native American people, customs, or events. The assessment of the focus of content used for instruction is one of the major concerns of multicultural curriculum transformation.

The issue of personnel profiles was addressed also by Oliver (1990) in her additional concerns for students whose secondary school experiences were just completed:

> Can you recall ever having a discussion with a teacher or other school staff member about the importance of learning about the diversity of people?

> Was there a person or group in your school that you believe was a special advocate for issues that particularly affect racial groups other than your own?

> Did you ever have the opportunity to interact with this person or group? If so, how were you influenced by that interaction?

> If there were students in your school of races other than your own, did you ever interact with them? If so, how?

H. Multicultural curriculum programming views inclusion, survival, and retention in programs of curriculum as the highest priorities, as opposed to exclusion and limited participation of learner—clients.

This basic principle of multicultural curriculum development relates directly to those programs where cultural difference is a recent phenomenon. It should be remembered that the multicultural transformation of our society emerged out of racial desegregation, which some consider the most critical event of the century.

America engaged in systematic exclusion of certain profiles from participation in many areas of our society, not because persons were unable or unwilling to participate, but because our policies—written and unwritten—prohibited their participation. For example, females in America were not considered eligible to exercise voting privileges for many years. Later, the *Constitution* had to be amended to grant such rights. So it was with many culturally different persons in the academic arena.

Many schools and school districts are still struggling with the practical and theoretical dimensions of having cultural difference as a common element of institutions, programs, practices, and curricula. Teacher education has also done little to deal with the prevailing perception that inclusion of cultural difference is not a good idea or practice. Our position is that one of the new principles of multicultural curriculum transformation involves a highly prioritized concern for the inclusion of different profiles of learners, teachers, and other staff in schooling centers where their presence has been a relatively recent event.

For example, if no Mexican American teachers have been members of a school staff in the past, the first such teacher becomes a kind of "trail blazer" in the evolution of equity for that program. It is important that such profiles be included in the teaching team. Often, a deliberate effort must be made to include such profiles, not just because Mexican American learners need the cultural reinforcement provided by the presence of that teacher, but because non-Mexican American learners need help in viewing that population as much as providers of academic services as they do consumers of such service.

I. Multicultural curriculum programming is not limited to the social sciences or to programs generally associated with "compensatory modeling."

Rather, it is concerned with comprehensive programming areas including procedures, instruction, policies, appraisal, assessment, personnel, materials, curriculum content emphasis, and the total ecology of the learning setting. Elsewhere, we have attempted to identify beginning steps for those interested in reprogramming the traditional disciplines (subjects) of the curriculum. The emphasis here, however, involves a more comprehensive curricular approach to upgrading what learners experience as part of their schooling. Our proposals include the following kinds of issues:

Recognizing the racial-ethnic history of the school curriculum in America. From the 1636 emphasis of the Boston Latin Grammar School curriculum, we now ask to what extent the curriculum leaves learners with a knowledge—and appreciation—of the presence and contributions of Native Americans, African Americans, Hispanic Americans, and Asian Americans?

Embracing alternatives to the way in which learning traditionally occurs in mass-produced educational programs. We must now consider the quantity of "teacher-talk" versus the quantity of learner action in their academic growth. Is there any other way that the learner can reach the academic objectives other than "listening to the teacher" and responding on a paper-pencil written test? While this system may be an important channel for present-day schooling, it is not the only way to learn. Multicultural curriculum transformation promotes alternatives to this tradition. The world is now seen through multiple lenses, not just one lens.

Reducing academic racism and/or sexism. We believe that education is a moral responsibility and that the mission of the curriculum is something more than just narrow concern with cognition. Academic racism exists when the practices associated with teaching and learning assume that the traditional intellectual inferiority or superiority of a student, faculty member, or staff member is based primarily on one's race, ethnic identity, or gender. It reflects an imbalance based on instructional preference which results in extremely limited learnings about racially and ethnically different persons, ideas, heritages, and events, or gender difference. Racism and sexism are a mixture of power, privilege, and prejudice which is reflected behaviorally.

Multicultural curriculum programming calls for institutional and public policy advocacy to eliminate racial, ethnic, and sexual discrimination. One size does not fit all is as true for curriculum as it is for any other area of our lives.

Another facet of multicultural curriculum programming is to assert that the ultimate mission of public education is to develop—within learners—the capacity to question others and to question answers, not just to answer questions. Education is not designed to promote dominance, but to promote the prominence of cultural difference. Overly narrow curriculum which attempts to respond to the "hour of crisis" is now considered dangerous for America's learners.

J. Multicultural curriculum programming demands clear perceptions of one's commitment to the elements of moral leadership in a society which offers glaring contradictions to many of its constituents.

Further, it recognizes that all human learners experience various stages of "ethnic readiness" to learn. (Readiness is extended to "gender readiness" as well as "economic readiness" in the schooling process). Multicultural education is a comprehensive curricular program which embraces cultural-ethnic differences as legitimate, basic foundational components of the schooling experience. It enhances the presence of racial, ethnic, linguistic, and economic variations through curriculum content and school policies, procedures, and practices—including practices of recognition, reward, and disciplinary action.

The instruction, counseling, administration, coaching, and communication all reflect diversity in implementation and assessment. Further the curriculum reflects the experiences, perspectives, cultural orientation, and mannerisms of culturally-different populations as well as others for whom the school program was originally designed. The programming has an obligation to be deliberate in embracing the diversity of populations enrolled in any given school, district, or program, but programming should never be limited to such enrollment.

Our position is that those responsible for school programs must clearly understand the level of their commitment to human service for all humans coming for those services. Many people are committed to providing curricular services for persons who are racially, economically, and linguistically like themselves. The commitment to provide educational services in cross-racial, cross-ethnic settings where the provider and client are different from each other must now be re-evaluated, because the absence of such commitment is detrimental to the development of a multicultural focus for the school curricula.

Critical Issue 6:
What about Learners and Their Survival?

The survival of culturally different learners in the academic center (school) is a major consideration for multicultural curriculum transformation. How does one survive any environment? Historically, survival has meant total conformity to the environment the way one finds it. Today, there is much less tolerance for total conformity in the academic environment. There is a quest for the institutions to "meet cultural difference halfway" in the process.

Schools and programs are being asked to change in light of the cultural difference brought by a more diverse population. Some might ask if we are "lowering standards" when we accommodate diversity. There is a definite difference in lowering standards and changing the perceptions and practices of curriculum implementation. Culturally different persons want to survive, but not at the cost of total denial of the cultural profile they bring to the learning center.

Part of the survival of the cultural self includes a recognition that what one learns in school about oneself is critical to the psychological well-being of the person. When one sees so few survivors in the cultural-academic mix of the American school, new questions arise among those concerned. Why do so many culturally different students become alienated from the traditional schooling process?

Sometimes the way policies are implemented may have major bearing on the way the school is viewed. At other times, it is clear personality differences and perception differences enter the process. But those responsible for multicultural upgrading of American curriculum must now attend to the survival of the culturally different.

In some circles, for example, ratings are being published regarding the survival of certain groups. The graduation rates of college athletes is one of the recent examples. Schools are now being rated (and the ratings published) on the basis of their rate of athletic graduation. In the rapidly changing school districts of America, such ratings will become more common regarding the retention and graduation of the culturally different.

When we speak of the culturally different, we refer to any population which (historically) was not part of the academic marketplace in large numbers. While this discussion is not focused on America's accommodation of the handicapped or physically challenged populations, it is interesting to note how America has attempted to include that group in the least restrictive environments with fewer barriers than ever before.

Multicultural curriculum reform is now asking for fewer barriers—psychological, curricular, and instructional—for those who bring a different presence to the classroom. Overall retention is one thing, but the retention of the culturally-different in disaggregated compilations can tell a completely different story about the degree of multicultural upgrading.

In some programs, inclusion is as far as the program planners have gone. There is little attention to the psychological accommodation of persons after they have been admitted to programs. Today, multicultural programming asks that the perceptions of participants who bring difference to the academic arena be a major consideration in planning, implementing, and assessment of curriculum at all levels.

Critical Issue 7: Is Commitment to Diversity That Essential?

We do not believe that any clear-thinking educator is ever interested in delivering a low-quality instructional (or other) service to America's school clients. Americans have spent so much time in quantifying cognitive competency that we lost touch with the need for professional commitment, especially across racial-ethnic-linguistic lines. In this case, commitment means to obligate oneself to a cause or goal or pledge one's work and beliefs to programmatic objectives. This involves a multicultural perspective.

A multicultural perspective and overview characterizing curriculum programs and human service delivery are intended to result in a society which is open, diverse in its framework, nonviolent, and supportive of all humanity, especially curriculum participants. Such commitment transfers into being emotionally impelled to the goals of equity. Unless teachers, administrators, librarians, counselors and other practitioners hold such commitment, multicultural programming will fail.

The reason that many persons look to the social sciences for leadership in equity is because some other areas of the curriculum (particularly the natural sciences and mathematics) have sometimes assumed a level of neutrality regarding issues of ethics and equity. We now call for all practitioners to embrace the commitment to equity in curriculum matters in all areas. Multicultural, multiethnic curriculum can only be effective when it is accompanied by culturally-sensitive instruction, appropriately diverse curriculum materials, and an understanding of the culturally-influenced learning styles brought daily to classrooms and other learning settings.

The American educator is a human service provider who is expected to function in a profession devoted to the enhancement of the quality of life for all learners. Such commitment includes the willingness to provide a "friendly confrontation" with stereotypes which impact options and opportunities for any and all groups. Such confrontation will also challenge some of the commitments educators have developed to traditional notions about Western civilization, but the confrontation may also be therapeutic as well as intellectually stimulating.

To be sure, multicultural programming embraces practical and theoretical elements of schooling. It now aspires to be the defining element of curriculum in America—the one which really operationalizes the notion of "liberty and justice for all."

Multicultural education is linked to school-wide improvement and has implications for all of the persons and aspects of curriculum. In particular it calls for reviewing and developing policies on diversity and setting priorities for diversity characterizing all schooling. To do less will result in graduates being less equipped than they should be to enter the workforce or to live as a fully-functioning adult in America in the next century.

For Further Thought

1. Why do you think the authors selected the issuing of a teaching credential or certificate as a critical issue?

2. Can you think of other critical issues of which practitioners should be aware?

3. What are the differences between ethnic and cultural studies, between multicultural and international studies?

4. Select three of the critical issues and prepare a set of arguments as to the complexities of these issues in providing a multicultural environment for all students.

References Cited

Banks, J.A. & Banks, C.A., (Eds.) (1995). *Handbook of research on multicultural education*, New York: Macmillan.

Hughes, E.M. (1990). Taking responsiblity for cultural diversity. *Black Issues in Higher Education*, 24-27.

Oliver, J.P (1991). *The relationship between the racial attitudes of white college freshmen and sophomores as influenced by exposure to multiculturalism in education practices*. Unpublished doctoral dissertation, Kansas State University, Manhattan, KS.

Other References

Banks, J.A. (1993). Multicultural education: Progress and prospects. *Phi Delta Kappan*, 21.

Banks, J.A. (1993). Multicultural education: Development, dimensions, and challenges. *Phi Delta Kappan*, 22-27.

Garcia, J. & Pugh, S.L. (1993). Multicultural education in teacher prepartion programs: A political or an educational concept? *Phi Delta Kappan*, 214-219.

Howard, G.R. (1994). Whites in multicultural education: Rethinking our role. *Phi Delta Kappan*, 36-41.

Pang, V.O. (1994). Why do we need this class? Multicultural education for teachers. *Phi Delta Kappan*, 289-292.

Price, H.B. (1992). Multiculturalism: Myths and realities. *Phi Delta Kappan*, 208-213.

Singer, A. (1994). Reflections on multiculturalism. *Phi Delta Kappan*, 284-288.

Notes

The absence
of instructional
vision results
in the absence
of social and
academic justice.

—James B. Boyer

Chapter 10

Relationships of Poverty and Learning in a Multicultural Society

Issues of Teaching and Learning with the Economically Poor

For some time, the American school has struggled with admitting that it has not been as functional or accommodating to an observable group of learners who are distinct because they emerge from families who are economically poor, even by government standards in America. Economic deprivation is a reality for millions of America's children. Some estimates indicate that twenty-five to thirty percent of the forty-five million school children in America come from such families. Changing economic patterns cause the numbers to fluctuate frequently, and because society has always turned to the schools for help in the solution of human problems, educational institutions must more directly address poverty in their programming.

There is a belief that corrective action regarding impoverished learners must be accompanied by a preventive instructional effort. These must be simultaneous if we are to adequately serve the economically poor populations of America's schools. First, there must be a recognition that the organized, mass-production schools of America are essentially "middle-class institutions" operated by members of the middle class, even if some of the participants recently emerged from economically poor families themselves.

As such, this "middle-class institution" has some difficulty seeing any strengths brought to the schools by economically poor learners or their families. This must become an immediate concern for multicultural curriculum programming. The perceptions of those who teach must be addressed. How are poor learners seen by the school? To what extent are they included in the reward systems of schools? To what extent are economically poor learners included in non-athletic school activities?

There is a culture of poverty which is characterized primarily by economic deprivation—moneylessness. The economically poor to which we refer are those experiencing the absence of financial resources which, in our society, is surely a disadvantage—but these families are not to be viewed as "deficits." At an earlier time, these families were referred to as "culturally deprived," but our position is that there are no culturally deprived persons or families.

No one is deprived of culture; culture is what helps to describe who we are and how we wish to be viewed. There are cultural differences, which implies that many economically poor persons differ in their style, perception, and approach to the school and its middle class identity as an institution. But we maintain that difference is not a deficit. Therefore, economically poor learners are not culturally deprived; they simply bring differences to the school which are not always embraced by school practitioners.

What Are Cultural Variations?

Economic deprivation may demand that economically poor families improvise in many areas of their lives, including the way they attempt to solve problems and undertake learning tasks. The lack of money precludes the purchase of many family experiences which the schools generally consider common to all families. Inherent in the notion of economic deprivation and the absence of money is the notion of academic and intellectual deprivation. We take the position that it is more a cultural variation than an academic and intellectual deprivation. If there is a culture of poverty, then that culture varies, in many ways, from the middle-class culture of the school.

Such variation can be more effectively accommodated by a multicultural transformation of the school and its programs.

No professional service is effective unless the service provider understands the client and his/her perception of the world, and of the service being provided. The following is intended to help professional educators comprehend this population better.

Many learners come to the school (at kindergarten or first grade level):

(1) Without ever having had a birthday party;

(2) Without ever having been on a family vacation;

(3) Without ever having been to a circus;

(4) Without ever having been to a parade;

(5) Without ever having been to a museum;

(6) Without ever having been shopping with their parents; and

(7) Without ever having had a story read to them.

All of these are experiences that have been known to contribute to the perceptual development of children. The lack of these and other social experiences during the pre-school years often leave such children less ready for the complexities of schooling than would otherwise be the case. Most learners from middle-class families have enjoyed all of these experiences prior to entering school. Culturally-sensitive instruction is now essential for effective service to such experience deprived populations.

Cultural sensitivity means having cognitive and effective concerns with poverty as a factor in the lives of children.

While our references to poverty and impoverished persons and families has been focused on family income, we recognize other indexes—such as health preservation, especially preventive health practices, quality of housing, food patterns, and transportation considerations. Additionally, the economically poor are more likely to have no savings and no economic security such as real estate, retirement programs or insurance, or other factors which reduce economic risks. They often make purchases in smaller amounts, getting less for their money than families with greater incomes. Many poor families, in attempting to meet their physical needs, resort to borrowing money through formal and informal sources and incurring the psychological and financial costs of such practices.

The culture of poverty is characterized by elements of "dependency" and degrees of unpredictableness. Many of the poor work very hard and have been steadily employed for many years, but their incomes rarely seem adequate to provide basic living expenses. Additionally, there is a feeling of helplessness that affects the social factors of their lives. A general lack of political influence results frequently in an apathetic approach to voting or to interacting with political factors or people affecting them locally and otherwise.

The working poor (distinct from the unemployed) are frequently characterized by:

Limited Formal Education

Thus they need multicultural transformation efforts to accommodate them more effectively. America is a nation of credential-conscious workers. Without high school diplomas, certificates, degrees, and other evidence of training or apprenticeship, a lower ceiling is placed on one's ultimate income.

Limited or Non-Existent Marketable Skills

Many household heads have had difficulty gaining employment because their work skills are at a level where there is low demand for the kinds of work they can best perform. The workforce today is characterized by lifelong learning, even for those who bring credentials to the workplace initially. Schooling, then, must address more directly the development of marketable skills and all the implications of that development within the multicultural context of American education.

Economic Vulnerability

The basic skills of consumer analysis, cost comparisons, and similar economic activities are not exercised as frequently as they are by other consumers, and the quality of living among the economically poor is negatively affected accordingly.

Limited Alternatives

The working poor are often employed in those jobs which are less creative, less complex, and which seldom vary. Further, nonworking social contacts seldom go beyond kinship and the immediate neighborhood.

More Humane Services for the Economically Poor Learner

There are many areas in which one may start to respond more effectively to the population under study. Despite the prevailing image of economically poor children, a serious professional educator is likely to find a great many children who are shy, afraid, nervous, insecure, sensitive, depressed, and discouraged—all this amid tremendous potential for succeeding with the curriculum of the school. Many have experienced failure early in their school careers because curriculum programming failed to adequately accommodate their styles, perceptions, and approaches to learning; in addition, they were faced with much content which was alien to them.

The alert educator must address himself or herself to detecting when discouragement accounts for low achievement, given the alien (monocultural) curriculum, and work to offset its impact. One of the concerns for the transformation is professional understanding of the magnitude of issues surrounding the learners' world.

Many economically poor learners who may have difficulty understanding the components of instruction as provided—and who might be termed "slow learners," may exhibit this relatively slow approach based on the formation of habits of attacking academic problems, and not necessarily on lack of ability. There is a difference between lack of ability and limited development of work and study habits. Poorly developed habits are far more frequently the case than many curriculum workers are ready to admit. Perhaps part of the solution would be to initiate help with the development of work and study habits by seeking to have learners understand the significance of these throughout life.

Some economically poor learners have had so little academic nurturing (both in and out of school) that their emotional health has not had the opportunity to be developed at the level expected by the school. These are not disturbed children in the usual sense of the word, but rather children having difficulty developing maximally their interpersonal skills. The skillful educator will understand that this kind of learner will depend heavily on the quality of effective behavior exhibited in the classroom or learning center for ego-building and ultimate achievement. Some researchers believe that economically poor children will learn anything that is taught—if they believe the teacher cares about them!

One of the limitations now being experienced by many educators working with the economically poor is that they feel that their responsibility is limited to the transmission of facts, knowledges, and skills. With the economically poor, the educational role is expanded to include the ability to inspire learners toward academic pursuits. Often, this competency is underdeveloped within the traditional roles of teacher preparation and ongoing staff development. It is a critical competency, however, and involves a major look inside oneself regardless of one's teaching specialty (elementary, secondary, or other specialization).

Such considerations must be made as they impact management of the learning environment, efforts at remediation, and all approaches to assessment and evaluation. This discussion is not intended to imply that all the changes needed with the economically poor must originate in the schools, but it does imply that the educator's role and the curriculum program's role needs to be greatly expanded.

Historically, the American school has not served this population very well. Consequently, the educator's response has been to psychologically "dismiss" the learner or to work at having the learner removed from one's teaching responsibility. It is widely believed by some that the number of referrals for special education, retardation, behavior disorders, etc., is the direct result of classroom teachers unwilling to upgrade their instructional efforts to meet the needs of economically poor learners. This is not an indictment, but rather a call for renewed assessment of our approaches to serving this population. If the schools are to reach their potential and/or stated goal of serving all the children of all the people, then we feel that a multicultural transformation is the appropriate direction, combined with culturally-sensitive instruction.

Much of the above discussion assumes a healthy respect for diversity by all who offer their services as professionals and paraprofessionals in the schools of the United States. This healthy respect for diversity includes the willingness to address and advance learners whose families exist within the poverty structure. Again, if education is a moral responsibility, then those of us who consider that aspect to be significant will approach serving poor learners with greater skill, compassion, and integrity.

For Further Thought

1. Do you believe there is a relationship between a child's social and economic level and learning or achievement? Why or why not?

2. Given a class of economically poor learners, list the concerns regarding their educational environment that you would have to address as their teacher. Discuss how you would address these concerns.

3. Describe the culture of poverty.

4. How does the quotation—"The absence of instructional vision results in the absence of social and academic justice" (Boyer)—relate to our society and its educational treatment of children of poverty?

Other References

Knapp, M. & Shields, P. (Eds.). (1991). *Better schooling for the children of poverty: Alternatives to conventional wisdom.* Berkeley, CA: McCutchan.

Kozol, J. (1992). *Savage inequalities; Children in America's schools.* New York: Crown.

Wayman, H., Felix, J., Anderson, J., & Baptiste, Jr., H.P. (1992). *Students at risk in at-risk schools: Improving environments for learning.* Newbury Park, CA:. Corwin Press.

Notes

There can be Unity
with Diversity.

—H. Prentice Baptiste, Jr.
(modified from Horace Kallen)

Chapter 11

Instructional Services Commensurate with a Multicultural Philosophy
(Ideas and Approaches)

A Philosophy of Flexibility

All professional human service delivery—including teaching, administration, counseling, library services, media services, tutorial services, mentoring, and facilitating—tends to emerge from the philosophical position held by those providing these services. Decisive instructional specialists (teachers) who serve in a multicultural society have the responsibility of making numerous choices. All academic pursuit involves one in thinking, believing, and perceiving. All of us who work in schools must make daily choices, and it is philosophy—our individual philosophy—which guides those choices.

In a society characterized by diversity such as is ours, the American school is in the process of transforming itself from a traditional, overly-structured institution to one of considerable flexibility. The greater the degree of flexibility, the greater the incidence of decision-making that can emerge from our philosophical bases.

The greater level of flexibility is consistent with more choices, more alternatives, indeed with a society characterized by diversity. Because our schools have been quite regimented, management by traditional rules has proven adequate for many who chose to offer their services in academia.

Today, the issue involves the philosophy of the practitioner more than it involves the nature and specificity of the rules by which we tend to operate schools. Whenever clients (students, workers, etc.) feel that the service providers often fail to humanize the decisions made, there is rejection of the services being offered. The philosophy of the service provider, then, becomes a key factor in the quality and effectiveness of the instructional services.

Even when the service provider and the clients are aligned according to race, ethnic identity, first language, gender, economic category, geographic category, and propensity toward learning, the philosophy of the service provider still guides the quality of delivery and the level of receptiveness exhibited by the clients. What we **believe** is critical to the academic and professional atmosphere of the instructional workplace for all participants. In other words, if service providers **believe** their clients can achieve and be successful, those clients will achieve and will be successful.

There are many educational examples of the foregoing, such as Jonathan Kozol, a white substitute teacher in the Boston Public schools, who provided effective learning experiences for young African American students; Jamie Escalante, a Bolivian, who provided successful learning experiences in calculus for Mexican American students; and Marva Collins, who started and succeeded with a school in Chicago for potential drop out students of lower socio-economic backgrounds. All of these settings have provided successful experiences for their clients.

What Is a Multicultural Philosophy?

Historically, philosophy has referred to the discipline which

has as its core logic, aesthetics, ethics, metaphysics, and episte-
mology. Our use of the philosophic concept involves the reflection of wisdom and a general understanding of the fundamental
beliefs underlying a sphere of activity or thought. This reflection
of understanding involves human relations, the ways in which
learning occurs, the images projected through the instructional
sequencing, the attitudes expressed by an individual or an
activity, and the level of calmness and judgment employed by
one in a professional role serving others.

A multicultural philosophy, then, dictates our view of the
institution of the school. Our multicultural philosophies serve as
value screens for decision-making. Are schools designed to
engage thinking in any one direction? Is the culture of the school
to be devoid of philosophic perspectives? To what extent are we
responsible for diversity impacting our philosophies? And to
what extent have we examined the concepts of equality and
democracy as components of our multicultural philosophy?

A multicultural philosophy may not always be quantified,
but it will always use logic as one of the tests of its appropriateness for teaching and learning. One cannot have a multicultural
philosophy if one still believes that old-line corporate culture,
traditional organizational culture, and agencies serving the
public will always remain as they have been, that is, with a
topdown perspective on who shall participate in making the
rules, enforcing the rules, and punishing nonconformists.

Davidman and Davidman (1994) discuss the significance of
a multicultural perspective and how instructional decision-
making is so heavily impacted by our beliefs and considerations:

> A multicultural perspective is a state of mind, a way of
> seeing and learning that is shaped by beliefs about
> multiculturalism in American history and culture....
> This belief system helps teachers see (a) that culture,
> race, gender, religion, socioeconomic status (SES), and
> exceptionality, in complex ways, are potentially power-
> ful variables in the learning process of individuals and

groups, and (b) that useful ideas can be gained from studying the cultural systems... p.7

While diversity must be imbedded in the philosophic framework of instructional services for a truly multicultural society, that diversity must also be reflected in the actual curriculum content and activities of a modern school program. One's point of view regarding multiculturalism, regarding people (all people), and regarding the teaching profession will influence all the major dimensions of instructional delivery.

Davidman and Davidman (1994) also point out that teachers who function from a multicultural perspective will want to demonstrate cultural sensitivity:

> The teacher who works with a multicultural perspective will want to be culturally sensitive to students and their families and, therefore, will become adept at collecting, interpreting, and making instructional and management decisions based on sociocultural data.

This level of philosophic undergirding will increase the chances of cultural continuity for all the clients who come for our services. Any client who is not given the opportunity to maintain cultural continuity—between the client's profile, view of the world, and tasks identified for them—will be unable to "philosophically connect" or "psychologically connect" with the goals usually identified by the service provider.

A multicultural perspective (interrelated with a multicultural philosophy) then remains critical and essential to the practitioner's effectiveness in service delivery.

What Are Instructional Perspectives?

Instructional perspectives are interrelated factors involved in the vision of teaching held by the professional practitioner engaged in pedagogical services to learners in schools. They are the totality of a mental view of the tasks of teaching and learning as well as the importance placed on these activities and experiences with the learners who come for instructional services. Equity, then, is a key component of the perspective which is appropriate for a multicultural society.

Equity involves the environment, conditions, and facilities for learning, the options and opportunities included in that environment, and the outcomes or results of program operation. If the outcomes or results are less than what is desired, then changes may need to occur in any one of the other elements of the equity considerations. Equity does not necessarily mean the same entities for all learners. It does mean that all entities must be assessed and appraised in light of the needs of the particular learners and especially in light of the outcomes or results of present practices. Multicultural considerations now impact the very structure of American schooling.

What Is an Instructional Behavior?

Instructional behavior is any action or response to intellectual stimulation offered by a professional individual seeking to enhance academic growth or development. It embraces cognition, physical energy, and verbal and nonverbal communication with those to be taught as well as with colleagues who would normally expect supportive academic citizenship in the discharge of one's pedagogical responsibilities with learners. Instructional behavior involves numerous skills employed by those who offer services.

The transformation of the school calls for a more sensitive reflection of many of these skills which school people use daily. Scarcella, in a chapter in *The Multicultural Classroom: Readings for Content-Area Teachers* (1992), calls for the following aspects of culturally-sensitive instructional feedback:

1. **Interpreting student feedback**: How teachers interpret the feedback given by students.

2. **Complimenting and criticizing**: What constitutes compliments and what constitutes criticism as interpreted by both teachers and students.

3. **Correcting students' errors**: How students value error correction.

4. **Requesting clarification**: How students make such requests and how teachers interpret such requests.

5. **Spotlighting**: How teachers call attention to an individual student's behavior in front of others; the teacher's use of singling out.

6. **Questioning and answering**: How questions are used by teachers to check student comprehension and how students answer these questions.

7. **Pausing**: How much time students need to respond to their teacher's questions; how fast the teacher and students interact.

Given the significance of individuality in a multicultural society, all these instructional behavioral skills will now need to be reassessed by individual teachers in quest of a more effective instructional delivery system. While Scarcella's (1992) focus was originally with language minority students, the behaviors are, in fact, universal in their application to instructional services.

It should be noted that the improved instructional delivery in a multicultural society does not mean that an individual school is multicultural, multiracial, or multiethnic, but it does suggest that all American schools are educating learners whose lives will be impacted by diversity in one way or another. Even if all the students and all the staff now represent one ethnic-racial-language profile, the school exists in a multicultural society. Therefore, the curriculum and instruction should reflect higher levels of diversity than ever before.

What Is Instructional Comprehension?

Instruction involves the passing of authoritative information, skills, concepts, and perspectives within a facilitative context. It is not limited to telling something to another person. It involves understanding and connecting with the learning underway. Those offering instructional services are charged with understanding the information, the skills, the concepts, and the perspectives of those undergoing instruction (the students). This is consistent with a society that embraces equalitarian values.

In the larger society, the customer is having more impact on the nature of services, on the nature of products for public consumption and use, and on the validity and appropriateness of same as seen by the customer. In the United States, we have programs to insure product safety from the work of the Food and Drug Administration to children's toys and clothing. In a multicultural society, efforts are always underway to prevent dictatorship styles in almost every category of life.

Instructional comprehension of services in a multicultural society, then, are being appraised in light of the appropriateness and alignment with the culture, perspective, and practical usefulness of those being served. To be sure, the stage of physical growth and intellectual development of those being served (learners) will always be a factor. Decisions must be made about the readiness and appropriateness emerging from these factors.

Our concern with instructional comprehension is the extent to which the professional educator understands the power, the impact, and the analysis of his or her work as delivered in a society deemed more culturally diverse than ever before. This includes both the structure of knowledge and the format, framework, and environment of its delivery. How much does one understand about the way in which one's teaching, advising, counseling, administration or other services can be interpreted by one's clients? It should also be noted that parents of America's school children are the real clients and that their offspring are extensions of that client-population.

What Is Instructional Respect for Diversity?

Respect for diversity is an element which involves the educator's view or level of respect for the presence of diversity in the learning setting—the classroom, the learning laboratory, the school, the reading group, etc. Respect involves giving special attention and significance to a reality, an idea, or a proposal. It also includes high regard or special regard for an entity. Further, it embraces consideration or esteem for such entity.

A truly multicultural society is based on respect for difference—as opposed to contempt for difference or viewing difference as a neutral element. Difference, also seen as a strength, is strongly embraced because of its capacity to bring enrichment to the teaching and learning underway. If there is an assumption that schooling brings no differences which should be respected and professionally treated, then the level of instructional communication is proportionately adversely affected and the level of intellectual success in grasping new ideas is thereby reduced.

Of What Significance Is Psychological Tone?

The most immediate behavior in schooling affecting learners is verbal behavior. Psychological tone refers to the way in which an educator talks and the impact of that language relationship to the learner's desire to grasp whatever is being taught or whatever services are being provided. The psychological tone is determined by whether instruction (or other services) appear to be invited, or requested, or commanded, or demanded.

Invitational instruction (based on the tone of voice, the quality of the verbal environment, the nature of affective outcomes of the nonverbal environment, etc.) provides the greatest level of choice for the learner and is perceived to be more effective in an age of options and alternatives. Teacher talk (while it should be reduced in a multicultural society) should also be laced with "invitations to learn" in a diverse classroom or learning setting.

What Is the Significance of Visual Stimulation?

One of the newer areas of research today involves broader understandings of visual literacy. Visual literacy suggests that visuals have a language of their own and that one's capacity to read and understand that language is associated with one's preferred learning style and/or approach. Visual stimulation represents an instructional element that utilizes sight (alone or in conjunction with sound) to enhance a learner's immediacy of learning. Associated with the explosion of technology, it is a deliberate approach of meeting the preferred learning styles or approaches of many more clients/learners.

Educators serving in professional roles in a multicultural society have an obligation to incorporate visual stimulation in instructional planning. Earlier, there was an assumption that the most appropriate learning for all learners occurred from extracting meaning from a printed page (books, etc.). Today, while that is still a heavily used format, visual stimulation is essential for meeting the learning mode of millions of others.

The entire advertising industry has advanced the use of visual stimulation more than any other area of our lives. Its success has caused almost every other industry to embrace the impact of visual learning (photographs, pictures, diagrams, designs, modules, etc.) to enhance learning in a multicultural society. For generations, educators have employed graphs, charts, maps, and tables to enhance comprehension. Today, visual stimulation expands such notions to embrace a host of other instructional endeavors.

What Are the Skills of Diversity?

A skill is the ability to use one's specific knowledge readily and effectively in the execution or performance of a task. Diversity, as seen here, involves functioning effectively in settings in which persons present represent different racial, ethnic, cultural, linguistic, and economic categories. Such functioning may be with colleagues, with those undergoing instruction, or with those delivering the instruction. Further, this involves the educator's level of cognition or one's information which was gained through experience or association. In the American school, it could involve management of the learning experiences, the content, the concepts to be learned, and the psychological processes of how learning occurs.

Adler (1993) in *Multicultural Communication Skills in the Classroom* focuses only on language learning of learners who do not bring what he calls standard language to the school or classroom. Our concern is encouraging the instructional team to build on whatever strengths the learner brings. Those strengths may be in language, in style, in forms of comprehension, or in preferences other than what the school has generally known. Adler points out that the school is a middle-class institution and has not served those well who are not so classified. His assessment, we think, is an accurate one—but we would challenge those providing instructional services to upgrade and/or reassess their basic skills of diversity in these times.

For Further Thought

1. Explain the importance of a multicultural philosophy and its role in guiding instructional behaviors.

2. List the components of an educational environment that are characterized by diversity. Are there any components of the educational environment not affected? Why or why not?

3. What do you think are the basic skills of diversity for a classroom teacher, school principal, school psychologist, school librarian, school counselor, and the school's secretary?

4. What does the quotation—"There can be Unity with Diversity" (Baptiste)—mean to you?

References Cited

Adler, S. (1993). *Multicultural communication skills in the classroom*. Needham Heights, MA: Allyn & Bacon.

Davidman, L. & Davidman, P.T. (1994). *Teaching with a multicultural perspective: A practical guide*. White Plains, NY: Longman.

Scarcella, R. (1992) Providing culturally sensitive feedback. In Richard-Amato, P.A. & Snow, M.A., (Eds.), *The multicultural classroom: Readings for content-area teachers*. White Plains, NY: Longman.

The quality
of learning
is directly related
to the substance
(content)
of curriculum
materials.

—James B. Boyer

Chapter 12

Diversity Issues
in Educational Research

Research Should Help All Learners

Educational research is an ongoing activity of many whose careers keep them associated with academia. While much of the educational research conducted in the United States is associated with institutions of higher education, there is an increasing level of research activity being undertaken by those working daily with pre-adult learners (children). Also, many of the institutions of higher education are attempting to form direct linkages with public and private schools in the conduct of research.

Much of the research undertaken by educational specialists in the past has attempted to adopt the traditional natural sciences approach to discovering new knowledge about humankind. In some ways, this is admirable, because some disciplines have been engaged in a particular design for generations.

However, our position raises questions about some of the research endeavors underway today. While we applaud the funding provided for this area of educational activity, we are concerned that the limitations placed on the broad area of research may provide data and images considered less useful and less accurate than some would view them. If one of the major purposes of academic research is to improve the quality of life of subjects (learners), then we place our priority with that purpose.

Our assessment of the value and conduct of educational research, then, involves the extent to which learners are being helped. It further involves the extent to which specific learners are being helped—the economically poor, those with a first language other than English, those who are racially-ethnically different from the masses, etc.

Expanding the Research Dimension

Multicultural concerns include the expanded definition and dimension of educational research. We support both quantitative and qualitative research efforts to provide greater insight into the academic arena.

Further, we support a new look at the following categories that lend themselves to educational research but which rarely get attention by educational practitioners:

Historical research. That which builds a chronology of persons, groups, or issues not normally studied by traditional researchers in the professional educational research community.

Descriptive research. That which defines a reality and offers findings which do not readily lend themselves to quantitative reporting though they may contribute to professional understanding of teaching, learning, or consumer issues.

Creative research. That which is the result of compositions in educational theatre, music, art, drama, photography, or other areas including poetry.

In addition to traditional experimental research activity, these categories may need to be employed or addressed far more frequently than before. If diversity is the foundational base for educational effort, then it must also be part of the research effort for educational purposes. Traditional experimental research designs have long had something of a monopoly on the conduct of educational research. In the future, multicultural concerns will include friendly confrontations with the assumption that historical, descriptive, or creative research designs have equal merit in attempting to generate new knowledge on which to base professional practice.

Additional Multicultural Research Dimensions

There are several critical dimensions of multicultural education which the research community (including action researchers in public schools) may need to embrace in order to remain a viable entity within the academic framework of American education. This is basically because American education is now being characterized by diversity in design, in foundation, and in implications. Boyer (1992) cited several of these dimensions:

1. Recognizing racial and ethnic identities;

2. Understanding diversity;

3. Multiple learning environments;

4. Relationship of issues to academic disciplines;

5. Human rights, social justice, and choice; and

6. Inclusion of diverse populations.

Add to these dimensions or concerns the continuing factors of policy, program, and procedures, and one realizes how critical it is for educational research to expand its parameters when discussing research production and research findings. There is agreement that those engaged in full time educational research have provided the academic community with much data. Most professions base their practice on the best available research findings and educational practitioners are no different in this respect. The practice, however, can be no more equitable than the research on which it is based.

Multicultural Education Research Consumption

To properly assess the consumption of educational research, we believe the following questions must be addressed:

Which research is consumed most by those who would offer their services in educational programs in America? Particularly those whose services are provided in multiethnic settings?

To what extent does this consumption of published research impact perspectives on teaching and learning?

To what extent is this kind of question raised in the preparation of new educational research specialists?

Are issues of curriculum bias and research assumptions, as they may negatively impact subjects (learners), given much consideration in the preparation of new researchers?

To what extent are the topics chosen for new research effort appraised in light of the probable outcomes?

The Educational Research Team: Composition and Perspectives

Because of the powerful impact of research findings in the education community, many groups are now becoming concerned about the composition of research teams that conceptualize, produce, and disseminate such findings. It is understood that much of the research produced in the educational community is used as a basis for public policy at the local, state and federal levels. Therefore, questions about diversity of research teams and diversity of perspectives emerging from those teams are becoming more specific and more comprehensive.

Authentic Research Versus Basic Research

The concern over composition of the research teams extends to similarly to viewing the research findings and assessing their implications. The issue of equity and the way in which findings are applied has caused some observers to ask about the appropriateness of such applications. Some would argue that research findings are "independent" of biography and perspective. We differ with that position—all professional service is somehow related to how the services providers see the activity, the purpose, the interaction, and the limitations of the endeavor. For this reason, distinctions are now being made between research projects.

A **basic research study** (of any design) is one conducted by persons about populations of which they are not a member. For example, an African American male who conducts research on a population of Asian American females can, at best, only produce a study which we term to be a basic research activity. He (the African

American male researcher) may feel that he is bringing total objectivity to such research activity, particularly if he has not known Asian American females at an earlier time in his life experiences or academic environment. His data may be quite clear, and he may have controlled for a number of variables, and he may have knowledge of many historical, cultural, or other factors. His study is still considered basic research (rather than authentic) because he is not an Asian American female nor of Asian descent himself. (Note: Some research practitioners challenge our use of the term basic research, but we take the position that the research effort can not be considered from multiple perspectives and, therefore, is basic.)

An **authentic research study** can only occur when a member of the research subjects (groups) being studied is a part of the research conceptualization team and involves himself or herself during the conduct of the study and the writing of the research report. This person (or persons) would bring a lifetime of that profile's experiences to the research activity. An Asian woman (if it is Asian American women being studied) would need to be part of the research team conducting the research on such women. This kind of analysis will be high priority for educational research in the future in a society characterized by diversity at the level of which we speak.

One of the primary concerns in addressing educational research in a multicultural society would be the essentially monocultural, basic nature of much educational research. This includes the materials used in treatment as well as in training new researchers for participation as career researchers. Much research still needs to be done on many topics not generally included. The role of culture, ethnicity, language, and economic background in impacting research activity is now being explored.

Educational research for a multicultural society has a critical role to play in expanding the perceptions now held by many in the academic community. Multicultural education becomes the fundamental framework through which much of this discussion must emerge. How is research activity viewed by the practitioner? How much significance is placed on the findings offered by many traditional researchers? What influences the research questions originally identified by educational researchers?

Given the agencies which fund educational research in America, from the National Institute of Education to the various foundations and the state governmental programs, those responsible for practical research in schools will need to explore the issues of diversity more extensively. We do not limit our concerns to the establishment of a research committee in school districts or individual schools, because much of that is already underway. We are suggesting a more fundamental analysis of the entire research community's work with regard to diversity and equity. School policies and established practices may need to prepare for a "friendly confrontation" with tradition.

Our discussion has focused more on people than any other entity. That is because the educational community is engaged in human service endeavors. People are more important than any other factor in a multicultural society.

Academic and Social Research

All academic and social research will reflect human preference on methodology, design, and perspective. The very choices made in conceptualizing a research study emerge from the preferences and perspectives of those engaged in the study. All findings, then, are proportionately affected.

We see educational research as an arm of all academic and social research because of its heavy reliance on human beings and their mental, emotional, intellectual, and physical properties. Some time ago, legal parameters were created to protect subjects or learners from being unduly exploited in the conduct of research. We applaud such steps, but we are aware of the possibilities for violating such policies—unintentionally as well as intentionally.

Evaluation and Research: A Distinction

Evaluation is the process of making judgments about people, programs, and processes. Educational evaluation primarily involves making judgments about people, their intellect, and their performance.

Research is the process of gathering data on which to make those judgments. This discussion has attempted to expand the notions about research processes. When we fail to understand these differences, we run the risk of engaging in curriculum bias and fraudulent research endeavor.

Urgent Areas of Needed Research

All persons who would offer instructional services are in need of different skills, concepts, knowledges, and behaviors to adequately meet the need of the current clientele. Among the most urgent skills and studies needed by educators of the future—which should be the targets of future research—are the following:

A. Studies on Culturally-Influenced Learning Styles

Teacher education embarked on a major task of exploring preferred learning styles of elementary learners as well as secondary learners some two decades ago. Much work was done in this arena, and the idea was to prepare teachers to provide instruction more aligned with the learning styles of those being taught. On further examination, almost none of this work focused on cultural and/or racial differences.

Our position is that both those institutions which claim a primary research function and those who pride themselves on practical pedagogy must explore approaches to learning which are characterized by race, ethnicity, economic class, and—in some instances—gender. Little has been done. For example, in what physical arrangements do many Mexican American learners prefer to engage in the learning activity? Most schools still use classrooms organized in rows with all students facing the teacher. Is this their preferred arrangement? Is it most appropriate? Much research needs to be done on factors such as these and on the best way to prepare teachers for such culturally-sensitive instructional response.

B. Studies on Academic Racism and Institutional Racism

Many researchers on teacher education are in total denial that academic racism exists. Academic racism exists when the practices associated with teaching and learning assume that the traditional intellectual inferiority or superiority of a student, faculty member, or staff member is based primarily on one's race or ethnic identity. It reflects an imbalance based on instructional preference which results in extremely limited learnings about racially and ethnically different persons, ideas, heritages, and events.

Few studies have been conducted on such factors because they engage the philosophical basis of what teaching and learning must embrace. (It gets down to the world view of those that teach and their understanding of the social ills of our society.) Institutional racism is the creation, implementation, and enforcement of a policy or program that, on initial examination, appears to be fair and equitable, but that categorically and adversely affects large groups of clients supposedly being served by that institution. The American school is one such institution which, though not intended to be racist in its policies, often produces that result. Teacher education needs major research in this area.

C. Studies on Human Sexuality and its Expressions

Because the American school is a composite of the larger society, it can no longer assume that its program and operation will occur in a vacuum. Human sexuality is a part of each human being's existence. However, many communities and many teacher preparation programs do not address this as a factor of the clients. A clearer understanding of its many manifestations and their implications must become a stronger part of the research within teacher education.

With the attention given to sexual harassment in today's schools and the early onset of sexual behavior by students, teachers must be better prepared to address such issues. Little is presently being done in research or in instruction on this category.

D. Studies on African American, Hispanic American, and Native American History, Literature, and Music

If demographic projections hold, the American pupil population will continue to become more diverse. Culturally different students are already claiming major irrelevance of the curriculum to their lives, their world, and their cultural orientation. At the same time, most teachers entering the profession do not come from these groups but will be teaching persons from these highly visible groups.

An increased level of literacy on the history, literature, music, and art of these groups will help address the issue of cultural accommodation. Research studies must be done on teacher education programs and how they should embrace such literacy.

E. Studies on Nonviolent Conflict Resolution
(skills of negotiation, classroom power-sharing, etc.).

Anyone who reads the papers, listens to the news, or works

in an academic institution is well aware of the increase in violent behavior emerging primarily from unresolved conflict between human beings. What skills are being provided in teacher education programs that address such issues? We need a major focus on research, instruction, and service that will prepare teachers to respond to a mentality of violence.

Many culturally different teachers are needed for areas such as these. We need skills of negotiation, of how to share classroom power, and how to respect a "minority opinion" on an issue. In most classrooms, the teacher holds all the power of decision-making and never shares it.

F. Studies on Biracial Learners

Except for two or three researchers, the teacher education literature has failed to explore the dynamics of teaching and learning with biracial learners. For many years, America was in denial that biracial learners existed.

Today, the increased numbers and the open dialogue on such profiles demand that teacher education begin exploratory research and instruction on how to best serve that population. It cannot occur, however, without the teacher's exploration of his or her personal beliefs about such profiles. Additionally, the socialization of such learners must become part of the teacher's understanding of the most appropriate instruction.

G. Studies on Academic Sexism and Institutional Sexism

Academic sexism occurs when instruction, curriculum, policies, programs, and practices assume that boys and girls will behave and respond in exactly the same ways. When this does not happen, one or the other is quietly but consistently penalized in the academic arena. While the American Association of University Women has published reports on how girls are short-changed in the American classroom, little has been done to restructure teacher education so that new practitioners provide a more balanced program of instruction.

Our contention is that males are significantly short-changed in the American classroom and that the absence of male teachers throughout the primary grades is a major barrier to the elimination of academic sexism. Research must be undertaken on the impact of such realities and then teacher preparation instruction must be upgraded based on the findings of such research.

H. Studies on the Racial History of Teachers, Gender History of Teachers, etc.

Little research has been done on the personal experiences of those who apply to join the ranks of American educators. Each person has a racial history that impacts the way they view race and all of its implications. This is more than a generic study of prejudice and discrimination. This is an analysis of the origins of one's personal values and the biographical impact of how one makes decisions and delivers instruction, especially when the student population may be racially different from the instructor.

Whatever parents and significant others told teachers during their growing years about racially-different people as well as themselves could have major impact on the way one delivers instruction. Few people study their racial history and almost none of this has been part of teacher education research, particularly as it impacts teaching philosophy.

I. Studies on the Impact of Poverty

Two decades ago, there were many studies on poverty and its reflections in the workplace and the school house. When the face of poverty changed to young families and senior citizens, few studies emerged.

Our position is that poor people who turn to the schools for the education of their children are looking for a more appropriate curriculum and a more sensitive level of instruction that respects impoverished families. Few studies are devoted to the economic status of families with children in schools. Such studies are sorely needed—not just to describe poverty, but to analyze its implications for teaching and learning.

J. Studies on Visual Literacy and the Impact of Images on Learners

Visual literacy involves learning from sight, which may or may not be accompanied with sound. It embraces "one picture is worth a thousand words."

While diagrams and photographs have been used for generations in the delivery of instruction, we are now proposing that research be conducted on the powerful impact of greater utilization of sight for instructional purposes. This is tied to the cultural orientation of those who come for instruction.

K. Studies on Cross-Racial, Cross-Ethnic Parent Conferencing

Most teacher education programs have embraced parent conferencing as a major portion of the teacher's professional responsibility. In cases where the teacher represents one race and the parents represent another, major difficulties have occurred during parent-teacher communication. The basic assumption is that parents and teachers are partners in the education of children.

In many communities, there is an adversarial relationship between parents and teachers, especially when cross-racial or cross-ethnic conferencing occurs. Research studies are needed to determine how teacher education can provide the skills necessary for non-adversarial teacher-parent conferencing.

L. Studies on Gender Equity
(Male and Female)

While Women's Studies (as a discipline) may be finding a place in the academic mainstream, our concern is that gender equity is much more than pointing out discrepancy in pay in the workplace or how the school executes its various "reward systems."

Our position is that gender equity studies should embrace higher levels of male-female communication and should include work on how teachers could reduce the confusion growing out of male-female behaviors within an academic environment.

M. Studies on Cross-Racial, Cross-Ethnic Teaching and Learning
(Instructional Dynamics,
Therapeutic Instructional Ideas)

For years, there was an assumption that any teacher could teach any learner anything so long as the teacher knew the content. We now know that that is an erroneous assumption. Instructional delivery is now much more personalized whenever it is offered in close proximity and in a context with which all learners can relate.

For instance, while girls might have difficulty believing they could be like the picture of Einstein, might not they envision themselves as a scientist if they see pictures of prominent female scientists along with Einstein? The same with students of color.

In electronic instruction, there is the need to communicate slightly differently. But whenever the instructor works in close proximity to learners (as in a classroom), the opportunity for "instructional distortion" is critically increased when teacher and learner represent different racial/ethnic groups. The instructional dynamics of this reality are rarely studied. Our call is for major studies on instructional dynamics and on therapeutic instruction for the teacher education profession.

N. Psychological Accommodation of Diverse Populations

Psychological accommodation involves factors of an instructional relationship, a strong invitation to learn, and the symbols which suggest that the learners are not just tolerated but celebrated. The psychological accommodation of learners across racial and ethnic lines will rest, in part, on the psychological health of both the teacher and the learner. They will engage in productive behaviors which will be perceived to be mutually desirable and beneficial to all participants. Gender will also be an issue in the complexity of such accommodation. Race and gender are such powerful variables that condition all relationships in all institutions.

Teacher education has assumed that the legal initiatives of school desegregation would take care of all such concerns. Now, we are suggesting that we need new channels of assessing the level of psychological accommodation felt by the learner. The psychological reference to instruction is, in part, a function of how the instructor feels about those being instructed. Are they worthy of being taught? How important does this set of learners appear to be to the future of America? Does the instructor feel that the learners are capable of engaging in the academic enterprise? We now need research and development on the psychological accommodation of diverse student populations in the American school. This should start with the preparation of teachers and administrators.

O. Studies on the Nature of Research Production and Policy Formation

There are several critical dimensions of multicultural education that the research community must embrace in order to upgrade itself to meet the level of diversity in America. Decisions about research topics, questioning the fallibility of research designs, and reaching conclusions about findings when the research team is not diverse are all major considerations for upgrading what teacher education uses as data for program substance and decisions.

Educational researchers must now ask new questions about the "approved" topics for a thesis, a dissertation, or a funded research project from a foundation or governmental agency. Who is conducting the research? What traditional limitations are placed on it? Why do we hold to such traditions that were established centuries ago? Are they infallible? These are not comfortable questions. Boyer (1992) has previously raised questions of multicultural concerns in educational research. We continue to raise some of the same questions.

Competencies for Research

Baptiste (1977, 1979, 1980) and Boyer (1985, 1989) cited competencies (see Figures 1 and 2) that should be a part of school districts' inservice programs and that address the behaviors and more appropriate parameters of teachers' instruction to avoid instructional discrimination. Baptiste, through his research, has identified eleven cognitive and eight affective competencies that all teachers should possess. Most important is the premise that school district programs that include these competencies will provide teachers characterized by a "cultural demeanor" which will make them more attractive and amenable to all students.

For Further Thought

1. How can we diversify educational research?

2. What is authentic research? Why is this kind of research so important in today's society?

3. Which do you think are the five most urgent areas of needed research? As a specialized educator (administrator, teacher, counselor, librarian, etc.), how can you facilitate appropriate research in your chosen five areas?

4. What can you do to expand the educational research dimensions?

Figure 1:
Cognitive Competencies for Acquiring Multiculturalism

Phase I

Cultural Pluralistic Society
↓
Groups of People

→ Contributions
→ Experiences
→ Inclusion

Groups of People

Acquire a knowledge of the cultural experience in both contemporary and historical settings of any two ethnic, racial, or cultural groups.

Demonstrate a basic knowledge of the contributions of minority groups in America to our society.

Assess relevance and feasibility of existing models that afford groups a way of gaining inclusion into today's society.

Phase II

Multicultural Education
↓
K-12 Structure

→ Curriculum
→ Materials
→ Environment
→ Strategies
→ Testing Language

Application

Identify current biases and deficiences in existing curriculum and in both commercial and teacher-prepared materials of instruction.

Recognize potential linguistic amd cultural biases of existing assessment instruments and procedures when prescribing a program of testing for the learner.

Acquire a thorough knowledge of the philosophy and theory concerning bilingual education and its application.

Acquire, evaluate, adapt, and develop materials appropriate to multicultural education.

Critique an educational environment to the extent of the measurable evidence of the environment representing a multicultural approach to education.

Acquire the skills for effective participation and utilization of the community.

Design, develop, and implement an instructional module using strategies and materials that will produce a module or unit that is multicultural, multiethnic, and multiracial.

Phase III

Multiculturalism

Rationale

Develop a rationale or model for the development and implementation of a curriculum reflective of cultural pluralism within the K-12 school and be able to defend it on a psychological, sociological, and cultural basis.

Figure 2
Affective Competencies for Acquiring Multiculturalism

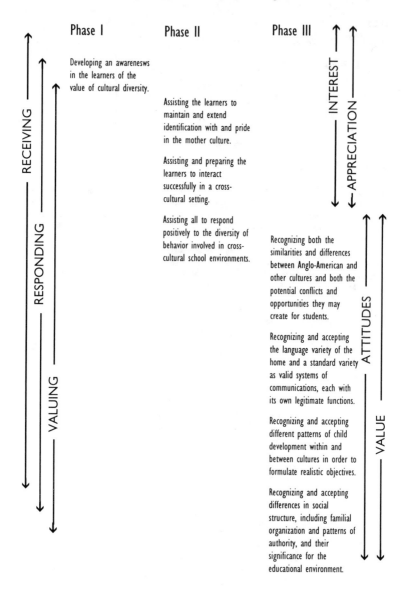

References Cited

Baptiste, Jr., H.P. (1977). Multicultural education evolvement at the University of Houston: A case study. In *Pluralism and the American teacher: Issues and case studies*. Washington, DC: American Association of Colleges for Teacher Education, 171-184.

Baptiste, Jr., H.P. & Baptiste, M.L. (1979). *Developing the multicultural process in classroom instruction: Competencies for teachers*. Washington, DC: University Press of America.

Baptiste, M.L. & Baptiste, Jr., H.P. (1980). *Competencies toward multiculturalism in multicultural teacher education: Preparing educators to provide educational equity,* Vol. 1. Washington, DC: American Association of Colleges for Teacher Education.

Boyer, J.B. (1985). *Multicultural education: Product or process*. (Reprinted 1991). New York: ERIC Center on Urban Education, Teachers' College, Columbia University (Now available through the College of Education, Kansas State University).

Boyer, J.B. (1989). *Collegiate instructional discrimination index. (multiethnic, multilingual, cross-racial, non-sexist)*. Manhattan, KS: Kansas State University, College of Education.

Boyer, J.B. (1992). Multicultural concerns in educational research. *Midwestern Educational Researcher*, 5 (2), Spring, 7-8.

Other References

Garcia, E. (1995). Educating Mexican American students: Theory, research, policy, and practice. In Banks, J.A. (Ed.), *Handbook of research on multicultural education*. New York: Simon & Schuster MacMillan.

Lee, C. & Slaughter-Defoe, D. (1995). Historical and sociocultural influences on African American education. In Banks, J.A. (Ed.), *Handbook of research on multicultural education*. New York: Simon & Schuster MacMillan.

Pang, V.O. (1995). Asia Pacific American students: A diverse and complex population. In Banks, J.A. (Ed.), *Handbook of research on multicultural education*. New York: Simon & Schuster MacMillan.

A curriculum
is not multicultural
if it does not have
social justice
as the foundational base.

—James B. Boyer
& H. Prentice Baptiste, Jr.

Chapter 13

Some Common Questions Raised by Practitioners about Multicultural Education

1. Gender Equity: Should We Have Single-Sex Schools in Our District?

While there is no denial of the negative impact of sexism as one of society's major social ills, this handbook has placed less emphasis on it than on some other topics—not because it is less important or significant, but because a number of other publications have chosen that as their only area of emphasis. In response to this question, however, we want to indicate that we consider gender equity to be of equal importance in the transformation of the American school and its programs. We feel that, at this time, there is a greater gender imbalance in schooling than any other area.

Also, because of the work of some feminist scholars, we have all been helped with our awareness of inconsistencies related to gender in instruction, in curriculum materials, in policy formation, in personnel assignments, and in values placed on humankind because of one's gender. Our position is that a multicultural transformation leads to the reduction and ultimate elimination of such ills.

Equity is a concept which embraces fairness, justice, and shared participation in American values and practices. It is an intellectual concept which manifests itself in behavioral practices impacting humanity at large. A mentality of equity would suggest impartiality as a way of life, a mode of practice, and a framework from which all else emerges.

Equity as a characteristic of American mentality would eliminate basic practices of discrimination (sex discrimination, race discrimination, age discrimination, economic discrimination, discrimination of exceptional persons with handicapping conditions, and others), exclusion, dishonesty, partiality, and distorted perceptions. The development of a mentality of equity requires some knowledge of and commitment to the high principles on which America was founded. The commitment, however, must be deliberately expanded to include those Americans historically excluded from full participation in all that America has to offer.

Gender equity seeks to eliminate the social ill of sexism in all its manifestations in American schooling, including curriculum materials, teacher behavior, administrative decision-making, counseling perceptions, etc.

The questions about single-sex schools emerged when some creatively thinking school people proposed such for African American males, a group for whom the schools had not functioned well. For example, in many schools serving this population, African American male students receive more disciplinary referrals, lower grades from teachers, are referred more often for special education (retardation) programs, and are suspended or expelled more than any other group in school.

Such school patterns are also consistent with America's prevailing concept of males in our society. For example, some ninety percent of all inmates are male. The single-sex school or single-sex class idea, then, is a response to some of the problems which persist in American education. Consider the following statistics:

More than ninety-five percent of all elementary teachers are female. (Some observers claim that this reality tends to negatively impact all male learners).

Roughly half of the elementary school student population is male, while in many schools there are no males on the professional or the non-certified staff.

Few males are in teacher preparation programs for elementary instruction, so the future does not look much better than the present for gender balance among the teaching staff.

While we recognize the study by the American Association of University Women that girls get short-changed in American schools, the facts support the demise of male academic performance and male psychological well-being in many other instances. The single-sex school, then, is designed to have a different kind of interactive dynamic occur during the schooling process. Some programs have proposed all-male classes with all-male instructors. We find this to be a remarkable effort toward reducing some of the academic and personal casualties of some of America's children.

2. How Do We Respond to Those Who Say It Reverses School Desegregation?

We are not proposing that all schools become single-sex schools or that every school have a single-sex class or two. We are suggesting that this become one of the options, among others, for serving a diverse population. In some districts, however, it is one of the alternatives for a better response to concerns based on gender. In Baltimore, there is one secondary school for females, although the faculty is composed of males and females. Ironically, it is also in Baltimore that the Robert W. Coleman Elementary School is experimenting with the all-male class with a male teacher. The strategy is to have such classes (single-sex learners) decrease the traditional competition across gender lines and to have teachers of the same gender serve as role models.

In Milwaukee, the public schools not only designed single-sex schools but included an emphasis on curriculum geared to African American males (the population for whom the program was initiated). While some observers are opposed to such creativity, our position is that existing programs have failed to decrease the incidence of conflict, of limited achievement, or of curriculum alienation.

It should be remembered that all such programs required some of the following:

1. Careful planning by professional staff, parents, and community leaders.

2. Well organized plans for admission to such programs.

3. Curriculum study which would address whether the curriculum program would differ in any way from the co-educational schools across the country.

4. Parental approval before a learner could be assigned to such programs.

5. Plans for constant review so that appropriate data could be generated for conducting meaningful evaluations.

6. The content of preparation of those who would serve as teachers, leaders, and support staff. Have they had studies specific to the gender or population in the school or class?

The single-sex school (or single-sex class) is designed also to help the learner with his or her education toward the goal of knowing oneself and one's heritage in the United States. Its most effective entities would include the promotion of relevant content to include the history, cultural heroes (and sheroes), the literature, the art, the music, the dance, and the total experiences of those like the learners. All-female schools or classes should emphasize the personal, political, economic, academic, and occupational perspectives of females in the United States. Authentic literature should be emphasized and particular mention should be made of the authorships of such works.

In an information society, the information is now more significant than ever in serving those who would consume it. Also, such programs should be committed to "expanding possibilities" for the clients. What else is there that women are not permitted to do in this society? How can such realities be changed?

3. What About Cross-Gender Instructional Services?

America has always had cross-gender instruction, but has done little research or development on its reality. There was an assumption that anyone who knows anything can teach it to someone else, and that gender was not a factor in such teaching or learning. Today, there is much research on mentoring and on the power of role modeling.

This new knowledge cannot be ignored or denied in a multicultural society devoted to equity for both genders. Our position is that the single-sex school creates a totally different environment which allows the learning to occur with less anxiety and with greater possibility for academic equity.

4. How Do We Respond to Those Who Say That Children Must Learn to Deal with Both Genders and Such Programs Impede Such Learning?

We find no evidence of persons who experienced education in a single-sex school having psychological or occupational problems following such experience. Nor is there evidence of persons who have attended parochial schools having difficulty relating to persons who attended public schools. These concerns end up being little more than "smoke screens" for those afraid to explore new avenues for transforming the American school.

5. What Is the Difference between Multicultural Education and Ethnic Studies?

Ethnic studies programs are those instructional programs which attempt to give equal attention to content drawn from the historical and sociological heritage of various identifiable groups such as the Native American, the African American, or the Hispanic American. Generally, the programs reflect the numerical strength of the group found in a given geographic area. Ethnic studies programs often limit themselves to the ethnic literacy about the groups under study. The basic intent of ethnic studies programs is usually to fill the literacy void created by the systematic curricular exclusion of these groups.

It should be pointed out that ethnic studies are not limited to identifiable groups such as those mentioned above; German Americans, Swedish Americans, and Italian Americans as well as others are often part of the conceptualization of ethnic studies programs. Some programs actually use the term "American Ethnic Studies Programs" to define their parameters. Also, many ethnic studies programs grew out of the move to desegregate the programs of American schooling.

Multicultural education programs place equal emphasis on ethnic and cultural expressions, their meanings and their implications. Using culture as the base, it explores the culture of major institutions serving broad populations. Multicultural education recognizes ethnic-racial identities and deals with the issues associated with such identities. It focuses on understanding diversity, multiple learning environments, overcoming perceived limitations in human value, and the relationship of issues to academic participation. While ethnic studies tend to focus on ethnic literacy as its major emphasis, multicultural education places more emphasis on social justice, inclusion, accommodation, and options-alternatives as the foundational bases of the educational enterprise.

6. What Is the Relationship between Multicultural Education and Cultural Competence?

Because of our concern for appropriate professional services in educational settings, we include the acquisition of cultural competence as a significant entity in the concept. Cultural competence is defined as the capacity or ability of an individual or program to provide services in ways that are acceptable and useful to clients because they make sense in terms of the client's expectations and cultural history.

Multicultural education values cultural differences as strengths, not as inconveniences or problems. It denies that difference is equivalent to deficits and it promotes the appreciation of human diversity in all of America's institutional programs.

While ethnic studies may describe instances in which a group under study has experienced discrimination or victimization, it does not generally place "corrective action" at the base of its intellectual investigation or discourse. Multicultural education, on the other hand, is deliberate in promoting its role as education for social justice, emphasizing that it is a process not just a product, that it is antiracist and antisexist, that it is for all students, that it is a liberating pedagogy, and that it requires change by all participants.

Willis (1993) has cited the following as part of the reason multicultural education is essential in these times:

> The achievements of European-Americans, including their art and literature, have been trumpeted, while those of other cultural groups have been overlooked.
>
> Such a limited view is unacceptable in a pluralistic democracy, experts contend. To correct this bias, multicultural education opens the curriculum to histories and perspectives of the many diverse groups that form America.

Multicultural education, then, tends to be a more comprehensive concept than ethnic studies in that it attacks the social ills of our society while restructuring schools and other major institutions serving all Americans. These social ills include racism, sexism, elitism, ageism, and any other practice which negatively impacts clients. Again, a program or curriculum is not multicultural if it does not have social justice as the foundational base because human rights within the United States can never be ignored.

For Further Thought

1. What do you think are the most common questions asked today by educational practitioners related to multicultural education?

2. How do you think gender equity complements equity concerns relating to race, ethnicity, language, and social class?

3. Do you think affirmative action has a worthwhile role in our society? Why or why not?

4. Can one implement a multicultural philosophy without some cultural competencies?

Reference Cited

Willis, S. (1993). Multicultural teaching. *Curriculum Update*, Association for Supervision and Curriculum Development, September, 1.

Other References

Bailey, S.M. & Campbell, P.B. (1992). Gender equity: The unexamined basic of school reform. *Stanford Law & Policy Review,* 4, 73-86.

Jimenez, E. & Lockheed, M.E. (1989). Enhancing girls' learning through single sex education: Evidence and a policy conundrum. *Educational Evaluation and Policy Analysis,* 11, 117-142.

Klein, S.S. & Ortman, P.E. (1994). Continuing the journey toward gender equity. *Educational Researcher,* 25, 13-21.

Lee, V.E. & Marks, H.M. (1992). Who goes where? Choice of single sex and coeducational independent secondary schools. *Sociology of Education,* 65 (3), 226-253.

Lockheed, M.E. & Lee, V.E. (1993). Single-sex and coeducational education. *International encyclopedia of education,* 2, 576-580.

Sadker, M. & Sadker, D. (1994). *Failing at fairness: How America's schools cheat girls*. New York: Charles Scribner's Sons.

Truely, W.G. (1991). The needs of African-American girls. *National NOW Times,* 23 (4), 4.

Tyack, D. & Hansot, E. (1990). *Learning together: A history of coeducation in American public schools*. New Haven, CT: Yale University Press and the Russell Sage Foundation.

Notes

...these strategies
should be
an integral part
of your daily
teaching activities.

—Cherry Gooden

Epilogue:
That's a Good Idea,
But...

The following is a discussion of some of the concerns voiced by teachers about the practicality of infusing multicultural concepts into their on-going classroom activities.

"That's a good idea but...
I already have enough to teach.
I just can't add another thing."

You **do** have a lot to teach, that is why we certainly want you to see multicultural education as an infusion of culturally pluralistic concepts and strategies into your **existing** program. We **don't** want you to think of multicultural education as "something" to be taught on Mondays and Thursdays from 9:00 to 9:30 am.

Rather, these strategies should be an integral part of your daily teaching activities. For example, you have to teach sequencing skills, so why not use a Mexican-American recipe for tacos as the content material for this lesson?

"That's a good idea but...
I don't really need this
because most of my children
are black [or white, or brown, etc.]."

You do have a lot to teach, that is why we certainly want you to incorporate a multicultural setting. You must provide the experiences to help your students become interculturally literate. Since students in monocultural settings rarely get a chance to interact in meaningful ways with culturally different others, misperceptions and inaccurate observations can be formed due to limited information.

You have a unique opportunity to correct ethnic/racial biases by providing your students with accurate information on the histories, lifestyles, and contributions of different ethnic/racial groups. You should seek out curricular experiences that will help make up for the deficits inherent in segregated classrooms and/or communities.

Further, teachers in multicultural settings cannot assume that because children "are with each other" daily, accurate and positive perceptions of culturally different others will be formed. Rather, careful guidance and use of culturally focused materials can ensure that proper attitudes develop as well as positive concepts of self.

"That's a good idea but...
I have to teach my low group to read.
Maybe I'll let my fast group do those activities—
that is, after they finish the basal reader."

Multicultural activities should not be viewed as supplementary activities or extra frills to be used when there is a "lull" in the regular classroom program. Rather, these activities should be utilized in such a way as to ensure skills and concepts are taught concurrently with respect to cultural diversity.

Most materials can be modified so that all learners can profit from their use. In fact, these activities can be so motivating and so good for building positive feeling about self, that the some-times reluctant learner gets a "new lease" on learning. So, try it, they'll like it—but better still, they'll learn from it.

"That's a good idea but...
My school's parents and/or principal would have a fit if I used stuff like that. They expect me to teach to the state proficiencies."

There may exist some reluctance on the part of many persons who view attempts to "multiculturalize" school experiences as wasteful or dangerous (tsk, tsk). However, we must educate them to the realities of life. Ours is a culturally pluralistic society and our children must be able to function comfortably within the various groups of which they are and will be a part.

Share the information we have given you at PTO and at faculty meetings. **Demonstrate** how you can teach skills and pluralistic concepts at the same time by adapting your content materials to reflect the cultural realities of society today. **Caution**: Don't preach, let your actions and successes speak for you.

—Source for "That's a Good Idea, But..."
Dr. Cherry Gooden, Texas Southern University

Reference Cited

Gooden, C. (1990). That's a good idea, but.... Unpublished manuscript. Houston, TX: Texas Southern University.

Other Reference

Willis, S. (1993). Multicultural Teaching. *Curriculum Update*, Association for Supervision and Curriculum Development.

Notes

Appendices

Appendix A

Martin Luther King, Jr.
The King Holiday – 3rd Monday in January

The King Holiday is America's only holiday devoted to the ideas and principles included in "Living the Dream" below:

"Living the Dream"

A day to celebrate the life and dream of Martin Luther King, Jr.

A day to reaffirm the American ideals of freedom, justice, and opportunity for all.

A day for love not hate, for understanding not anger, for peace not war.

A day for the family: to share together, to reach out to relatives and friends, and to mend broken relationships.

A day when people of all races, religions, classes, and stations in life put aside their differences and join in a spirit of togetherness.

A day for our nation to pay tribute to Martin Luther King, Jr., who awakened in us the best qualities of the American spirit.

A day for nations of the world to cease all violent actions, seek non-violent solutions, and demonstrate that peace is not just a dream, but a real possibility, if only for one day.

If for only one day, each of us serves as a drum major for justice and peace, then we will bring to life the inspiring vision of freedom which Martin "Dreamed."

—Source: Martin Luther King, Jr., Institute, Atlanta, Georgia

Appendix B

Administrator's Checklist
For Enhancing Multicultural Curriculum
(Multi-Ethnic, Non-Sexist)

A Practical Self-Test and Guide to Curriculum Development
for Multiculturalism in Schools and Colleges
(Toward Eliminating Racism, Sexism, Elitism,
and Ageism in the Totality of the Curriculum)

By James B. Boyer
Professor and Multicultural Curriculum Specialist
College of Education, Kansas State University
Manhattan, Kansas 66506

Boyer's Multicultural Curriculum Checklist

Multicultural Curriculum

Multicultural Curriculum incorporates the anthropological concept of culture and includes the physiological, psychological, sociological dimensions of a group of people. This particularly includes instructional sequences which attempt to reflect the totality of American culture, not through assimilation, but through acculturation and visible distinction of one cultural variation from another. Multicultural Curriculum addresses both the **similarities** and **differences** among people within the framework of equal respect for such differences. More specifically, Multicultural Curriculum (1) incorporates content data about highly visible minorities (Black Americans, Mexican Americans, Puerto Ricans, Native Americans, Asian Americans) as well as others, (2) includes an understanding of the Third World concepts, (3) recognizes content which is not of European origin, (4) specifically emphasizes intergroup relations, and (5) recognizes varied sources of content while reviewing existing curriculum materials (textbooks, film, library books, etc.) for their ethnic diversity and/or objectivity.

Administrative Function

Administrative-supervisory leadership in curricular thrusts can never be underestimated or replaced. Those educators who are assigned leadership roles have a unique responsibility for working toward particular thrusts, especially when those thrusts are not always understood by those who work with them. Persons in leadership roles are now being called on to assist in enhancing the broad concepts of multicultural curriculum in schooling at all levels (elementary, secondary, and postsecondary). Such curricular thrust is needed even if all those enrolled in the schools are of European background (that is, even if no minorities are enrolled in the schools).

The Administrator

For this Checklist, an administrator is anyone who has managerial or developmental responsibility for (a) curriculum, (b) personnel, and/or (c) budgetary concerns related to public or private schools. While there are many administrators who do not **directly** implement the pupil learning program, the influence of all school people is reflected in the **substance** of curricular learnings. The following Checklist is offered as a Self-Test for school administrators (including Principals, Superintendents, Supervisors, Curriculum Assistants, Subject-Matter Specialists-Consultants, Librarians, Deans, and Presidents) whose work help to shape the **real learnings** of students in our schools.

As an Administrator:

1. Am I well informed of the broad concepts of multicultural curriculum entities including the historical sociological development?
2. Do I consciously avoid implying the "**deficit model**" in supporting multicultural curriculum?
3. Do I encourage teachers and others to experiment and "be creative" in quest of higher levels of multicultural curricu-

lum effort? If so, in what ways?

4. Am I prepared to work toward resolving conflict among staff persons and teachers who may disagree on the concepts and procedures of multicultural curriculum?

5. Do I arrange time for teachers and staff to work on curriculum development efforts which would enhance the thrusts of multicultural curriculum?

6. Are there professional opportunities (conferences, meetings, etc.) which teachers may attend that expand the multicultural effort in the program for which I am responsible?

7. Do I provide Evaluative Criteria for teachers and staff to assess the multicultural impact on the curriculum?

8. Have I examined the hallways, walls, libraries, and other parts of the buildings in my school(s) to discover if the photographs, portraits, etc. there are reflective of the multicultural entity?

9. Are the photographs, materials, and other visible items **in my office** reflective of the multicultural curriculum?

10. Have I communicated how strongly I feel that multicultural curriculum is appropriate despite the percentage of racially/culturally diverse learners enrolled in my school? In my district?

11. Have I specifically communicated with the **Librarian** about the acquisition of instructional materials which would enhance the multicultural curriculum?

12. Do I suggest that the Professional Library (Teachers' Reading Center) in my school specifically include multicultural professional journals and books?

13. Do I schedule **Professional Faculty Meetings** during which the multicultural emphasis will be reviewed?

14. Do I provide direct help in assisting teachers to coordinate various **disciplines** in quest of the multicultural thrust?

15. Do I suggest that the school program use **current resources** (newspapers, television, human resources, etc.)?

16. Do I review the **student activities** program (band/choral music, athletic program, Library Club, Honor Societies, etc.) in quest of multicultural emphasis?

17. Do I raise the issue of **cultural diversity** with regard to the school lunch menus—in quest of total curricular development?
18. Do I provide opportunities for teachers and staff to **share successes and difficulties** in implementing multicultural curriculum?
19. Do I lead the staff effort to review the **Test Program** (standardized tests, teacher-made tests, etc.) in light of multicultural awareness, content, and instruction?
20. Are standardized tests given on Jewish holidays?
21. Has the issue of January 15 (Martin Luther King, Jr.'s Birthday) becoming a school holiday been discussed in your school?
22. Do I provide time for **instructional materials development?** (Also assessing for stereotypes? For authenticity?)
23. Do I review the economic levels of those learners who are suspended, punished, sent to the Principal's office, etc.?
24. Do I specifically work at **giving visibility** to those teachers who make particular effort to enhance the multicultural entity in curriculum? (Reward System)?
25. Do I suggest that the multicultural emphasis become **program content** for PTA meetings and the like? Do I work at helping to communicate the multicultural curriculum to parents and the community? If so, how?

Additional Multi-Ethnic Concerns:

26. Am I familiar with the Council on Interracial Books for Children? (1841 Broadway, New York, NY 10023)
27. Am I familiar with the Japanese American Curriculum Project? (P. O. Box 367, San Mateo, CA 94401)
28. Am I familiar with "Test Your Textbooks for Racism Rating" and other Viewpoint Newsletters from Foundation for Change? (1619 Broadway, New York, NY 10019)
29. Am I familiar with Curriculum Guidelines for Multiethnic Education? (Position Statement, National Council for Social Studies, 1515 Wilson Blvd., Arlington, VA 22209)
30. Am I familiar with the Mexican American Curriculum Office and its compilation of materials on Mexican Americans? (c/o

Xerox, Book Catalogs Dept., 300 North Zeeb Road, Ann Arbor, MI 48106).

31. Am I familiar with the American Library Association's Bibliographic Materials on Multi-ethnic Media? (ALA, 50 E. Huron Street, Chicago, IL 60611)

32. Am I familiar with Textbooks and the American Indian (by Jeanette Henry)? (c/o The Indian Historian, 1451 Masonic Avenue, San Francisco, CA 94117).

33. Am I familiar with national efforts to improve all aspects of children's literature?

34. Am I familiar with the work of the Human Relations Division of the National Education Association? (1201 Sixteenth Street, N.W., Washington, DC 20036).

35. Am I familiar with the nature of—and impact of—Bilingualism in schooling? (See *Learning in Two Languages*, a Phi Delta Kappa Fastback by Ricardo Garcia).

36. Am I familiar with Evaluative Criteria for Multi-Racial, Multi-Ethnic Education? (National Study of School Evaluation, Arlington, VA).

37. Am I familiar with the Association for the Study of Afro-American Life and History? (140l Fourteenth Street, N. W., Washington, DC)

Boyer's Multi-Ethnic Instructional Concept

Objectives	Content	Outcomes
(Skills, Concepts, Behaviors)	(Materials, Knowledges)	(Achievement, Understandings)

Ethnic Diversity

The Checklist is intended as an awareness and behavioral guide for those administrator-supervisors who have (or are developing) a commitment to the elimination of racism, elitism, sexism, and ageism. Administrative philosophy and perception regarding the **substance of curriculum** *are extremely significant factors in the ultimate quality of life (childhood life and adult life) in America.*

Appendix C

Boyer's Elementary-Secondary Multicultural Instructional Inventory
(Multi-Ethnic, Multilingual, Cross-Racial, Non-Sexist)
(Toward Eliminating Racism, Sexism, Elitism and Ageism in the Totality of the Curriculum)

By James B. Boyer, Ph.D.
Professor, Curriculum & American Ethnic Studies
Kansas State University

The delivery of instruction with a multicultural perspective assumes that professional educators embrace a commitment to equity in all its dimensions. The elimination of racism, sexism, elitism, and ageism is critical to the development of the kind of society which embraces differences consistent with the American ideal. Children in American schools deserve instruction which is characterized by a multicultural consciousness, by ethnic literacy, and by a growing appreciation for the existence, growth, and development of learners representing various ethnic, racial, economic, linguistic, and gender profiles.

Many of the items of this Inventory imply that issues of instruction will involve cross-racial, cross-ethnic teaching and learning. This inventory takes the position that no learner should experience instruction which does not value one's ethnic identity and profile. It also assumes that there is no one monolithic America and that instruction recognizes cultural reality and its meaning for achievement in American education.

Basic Multicultural Instructional Assumptions:

It is assumed that multicultural instructional delivery embraces more than a body of content but includes a pluralistic teaching style. It also assumes that professional educators are committed to moving American education from an ethnocentric view to a multicultural view.

It is felt that multicultural instructional perspectives transform life in schools so that we significantly decrease tendencies toward exploitation, oppression, discrimination, and victimization of America's children on matters over which they have no control—such as their race, language, gender, ethnicity, age, or cultural orientation.

Culturally-Sensitive Instruction:

Culturally-sensitive instruction with elementary-secondary learners (especially including middle-school learners) will reflect a professional knowledge base about adolescence and childhood but will also embrace ethnic considerations which avoid offending the culture, race, ethnic identity, age, gender, or handicapping condition of any learner. Such culturally-influenced instruction reflects a strong commitment to achievement but works at it through a sense of **achievement motivation**— especially on the part of culturally-different students. Culturally-sensitive instruction cannot occur unless the teacher/instructor **embraces a belief in education equity** and that **all children can learn**.

Multicultural Instruction Inventory

As a **Professional Educator/Instructor**:

1. Do I recognize that my instructional efforts (when providing instruction for persons culturally-different from myself) may be viewed as adversarial?
2. Do I understand that multicultural curriculum may be viewed as academically detrimental to America's educational future?
3. Do I understand that multicultural curriculum is designed to assist in the transformation of our society from a mono-ethnic, monocultural perspective to one which embraces the development of **all** Americans?
4. Do I recognize that multicultural education brings us into the realization that our **investment in people** is the ultimate investment in the future? Multicultural education draws its

foundation from people (students, educators, parents) as well as from the major documents of the United States (*Constitution, Bill of Rights, Declaration of Independence*, etc.).

5. Am I aware that multicultural education seeks to have professional educators **avoid being intimidated** by cultural differences among learners or other educators? At the same time, sensitive instruction is **not indifferent to cultural differences**.

6. Do I feel that I share a partnership in the quest for successful transition of the curriculum from monocultural, monoracial frameworks to a multicultural, multiethnic, gender-balanced framework?

7. As an educator, do I promptly intervene when the use of derogatory or disrespectful language occurs in classrooms which victimizes any human profile?

8. As a teacher, do I possess the skill to turn a racial/ethnic confrontation into a constructive learning experience for all concerned?

9. As a teacher, do I search for ways to reduce reluctance of students to discuss racial/ethnic questions? (These are frequently known as anxiety reduction practices).

10. As an educator, am I aware that my instructional manner must communicate a belief that all learners (including the culturally-different learners) are capable of meaningful academic achievement?

11. As an educator, do I regard race relations or **ethnic relations** as an aspect of the entire school curriculum rather than as a single **problem area**?

12. If I have relatively few students racially/ethnically unlike myself, do I tend to **interpret their learning behavior** as negative rather than as cultural expressions?

13. As an educator, do I refrain from all derogatory racial, ethnic, religious jokes or negative observations when working with the class group? (Even if my students have engaged in such behavior?)

14. As an educator, do I understand that I am responsible for the

psychological tone (ecological structure) of the pluralistic classroom?

15. As a teacher, do I employ professional literature and/or research findings to assist in understanding culturally-different learners? (This is extended to understanding bilingual learners, biracial learners, and learners with handicaps or exceptionalities).

16. Do I emphasize **student success** rather than student failure—especially in cross-racial or cross-ethnic settings ?

17. Do I expect and encourage high academic effort from culturally-different learners with full understanding of the differences in learning styles which are racially or culturally influenced?

18. Am I skilled in varying lesson plans so that they capitalize on ethnic/racial considerations that arise in the classroom?

19. Do I call on the culturally-different learners in class as frequently and with as much "academic intensity" and respect as I do the learners who do not represent that cultural difference?

20. Am I skillful in any disciplinary practices which reflect a consciousness of ethnic/cultural identification on the part of the learners?

Multicultural Curriculum Management

21. Do I use bulletin boards, posters, photographs, maps, and other curriculum materials to enhance student understanding of people, information, and issues commonly excluded from textbooks and other curriculum materials?

22. Do I design learning activities around identifying bias found in textbooks, television, mass media, library materials, magazines, and newspapers?

23. Do I ask learners to rewrite or update materials which have excluded certain ethnic/racial profiles from their learning materials?

24. Do I point out to students the sexist or racist bias of books or other curriculum materials? Do I help them to identify bias

and important omissions in materials and institutions?

25. Do I develop or locate supplementary materials which enhance a more balanced curricular experience for learners in my classroom?

26. Do I invite local resource persons or others into my classroom to provide newer levels of diversity while enriching the curricular experience normally provided?

27. Have I checked to see if materials from which reading instruction emerges contain characters who represent high profile ethnic/racial populations like African American people, Asian American people, Native American people, or Hispanic people?

28. Do I assign student papers, writing exercises, projects, and other learning activities to deal with topics traditionally omitted from school learning material?

29. As an educator, do I seek to develop a collection of non-racist, non-sexist literature and other materials for my students? Also, do I seek to identify books that students may be encouraged to use?

30. Do I encourage students to examine the impact of their behavior as members of groups—and in groups of diverse students? (This is intended to help students discover that **their way** of doing and thinking is **not the only way** nor is it always the **best way**.)

31. Do I work to develop my comprehension of Women's Studies—because they have been traditionally excluded from curriculum content?

32. Am I conscious of the need for multicultural enhancement to examine the issues involved in human relationships across racial-ethnic lines? (Note: Teacher knowledge of diverse profiles can be enriched by having students grow in their ethnic literacy).

33. Do I seek to have my students express, maintain, and celebrate cultural differences and racial differences? (Celebration is beyond toleration).

34. Do I, as an educator, insist upon behavior which is neither

hostile to any other group, or which perpetuates stereotypes of the culturally different?

35. Are any procedures, rules, or regulations of my classroom perceived to be unfair by culturally-different students? Does this population feel that the learning setting is an experience in being overly-monitored?

36. Do I recognize holidays which are especially significant for the culturally-different populations in my program?

37. Do I administer tests on Jewish holidays? On *Cinco de Mayo*? (Groups of students may observe some holidays not recognized by those who prepare school calendars.)

38. Do I work especially to have pluralistic values enhanced through my instructional delivery? (This includes using materials written **by** culturally-different authors—and about culturally-diverse populations)?

39. Do I make suggestions to the Librarian or Media Specialist for enhancing the school's materials collection toward a multicultural, multiethnic level?

40. Do I use current resources (newspapers, television, human resources) which reflect the diverse nature of the United States?

Appendix D

Basic Administrative Competencies for Multicultural Settings

While many administrative programs are attempting to review elements which might address such competencies, the following listing is basic to the establishment of multicultural programmatic concerns:

1. Administrative awareness of federal, state, and local laws and

legislation directly affecting specific ethnic, racial, or other groups.

2. Administrative awareness of agency and/or organizational policy which reflect racial, ethnic, or other inconsistencies that are perceived as biases against such groups.

3. Administrative commitment to the deletion of any policy, practice, or guideline which may be an outgrowth of institutional racism and which may be perceived as such by pluralistic populations.

4. Administrative design and support of academic programs which highlight "success stories" of various ethnic groups and which denounce differences which are seen as deficits.

5. Administrative awareness of the customs and traditions held in high esteem by members of various ethnic groups—particularly those which may be viewed by traditional administrators as being in conflict with "tradition."

6. Administrative skill in establishing and monitoring staff development programs which enhance human relations in racially-ethnically-economically diverse student/staff settings. (While this is critical for all administrative functioning, it is especially significant for those offering their services in areas in which ethnic/racial minorities are heavily represented.)

7. Administrative competencies of listening (really listening) as well as speaking in their daily communicative styles. Considering the "oral tradition" of many ethnic groups, the competent multicultural administrator must listen for statements as well as the implications of those statements from subordinates, students, and the public.

8. Administrative resourcefulness in providing information to faculty, staff, and students on highly visible ethnic, racial, and cultural groups represented in the United States, and particularly those who are the most recent arrivals. (Example: Haitians and similar groups).

9. Administrative involvement in enhancing ethnic history, ethnic music, ethnic artistic expression, and the total ele-

ments which provide cultural identity and cultural satisfaction for persons who have been perceived as something other than "assets to society."

10. Assertive styles in informing populations of their legal rights and the rights of others in culturally pluralistic societies. It is understood that rights and responsibilities are concomitant elements.

11. Administrative influence in recommending the employment of faculty, staff, and resource persons who reflect the ethnic/racial makeup of the region—and particularly the school or program. (This is essential for modeling and for authenticity).

12. Administrative leadership in the identification, selection, acquisition, and utilization of curriculum materials which are nonracist, nonsexist, nonelitist, and which are inclusive of the human variation of our society.

Educational change and educational development are always based on the graphic need to better serve those who are clients of educational programs. Such needs are (for academic leadership/management) inextricably tied to ethnic/racial/economic identity.

Shirley Napier in "Multicultural Education: A Concept Paper" (ERIC: ED-17742) cites several points for top administrators, one of which is the educational re-organization for accommodating culturally pluralistic approaches to service delivery.

If administrative services are to keep pace with the increasing numbers of agencies, institutions, and educational programs whose populations are becoming more racially and ethnically diverse, then a more rigorous and culturally refined set of competencies must become common goals for the preparation of those who would offer their services as leaders, managers, researchers, and practitioners for public educational programs.

Bibliography

References Cited

Adler, S. (1993). *Multicultural communication skills in the classroom.* Needham Heights, MA: Allyn & Bacon.

Anderson, J.A. (1988). Cognitive styles and multicultural populations. *Journal of Teacher Education 5*, 2-9.

Archer, C. (1990). *Living with strangers in the USA.* Englewood Cliffs, NJ: Prentice Hall.

Banks, J.A., (Ed.) (1973). *Teaching ethnic studies.* Washington, DC: National Council for the Social Studies.

Banks, J.A. (1977). The implications of multicultural education for teacher education. In Klassen, F. & Gollnick, D. (eds.), *Pluralism and the American teacher: Issues and case studies.* Washington, DC: American Association of Colleges for Teacher Education, 1-30.

Banks, J.A. (1991). *Teaching strategies for ethnic studies.* Boston, MA: Allyn & Bacon.

Banks, J.A. & Banks, C.A. (1993). *Multicultural education: Issues and perspectives. Massachusetts.* Boston. MA: Allyn & Bacon.

Banks, J.A & Banks, C.A., (Eds.) (1995). *Handbook of research on multicultural education.* New York: Macmillan.

Baptiste, Jr., H.P. (1977). Multicultural education evolvement at the University of Houston: A case study. In *Pluralism and the American teacher: Issues and case studies.* Washington, DC: American Association of Colleges for Teacher Education, 171-194.

Baptiste, Jr., H.P. (1983). Internalizing the concept of multiculturalism. In Samucla, R.O. & Woods, S.L. (Eds.), *Perspectives in Immigrant and Minority Education.* Washington, DC: University Press of America, 294-308.

Baptiste, Jr., H.P. (1990). *Leadership, equity. and school effectiveness.* London, United Kingdom: Sage.

Baptiste, Jr., H.P. (1994). The multicultural environment of schools: Implications to leaders. In Hughes, L.W. (Ed.), *The Principal as leader.* New York: Merrill/MacMillan, 89-104.

Baptiste, Jr., H.P. (1995). Definition of multicultural education. Proposed comprehensive remedial plan and order for the Rockford School District, Rockford, IL.

Baptiste, Jr., H.P. & Archer, C. (1994). A comprehensive multicultural teacher education program: An idea whose time has come. In Atwater, M., *et al.* (Eds.), *Multicultural education: Inclusion of all.* Athens, GA: University of

Georgia, 65-90.

Baptiste, Jr., H.P. & Baptiste, M.L. (1979). *Developing the multicultural process in classroom instruction: Competencies for teachers*. Washington, DC: University Press of America.

Baptiste, Jr., H.P., Baptiste, M.L., & Gollnick, D.M. (1980). *Multicultural teacher education: Preparing educators to provide educational equity*. Volume 1. Washington, DC: American Association of Colleges for Teacher Education.

Baptiste, M.L. & Baptiste, Jr., H.P. (1980). *Competencies toward multiculturalism in multicultural teacher education: Preparing educators to provide educational equity, Volume 1*. Washington, DC: American Association of Colleges for Teacher Education.

Barna, L.M. & Jain, N.C. (1978). Teaching of intercultural communication at the undergraduate and graduate levels. In *Overview of intercultural education, training and research*, Hoopes, D.S., Pedersen, P.B. & Renwick, G.W. (Eds.), Vol. 2, *Education and training*. Washington, DC: Society for Intercultural Education, Training, and Research.

Baruth, L.G. & Manning, M.L. (1992). *Multicultural education of children and adolescents*. Needham Heights, MA: Allyn & Bacon.

Bennett, C.I. (1990). *Comprehensive multicultural education: Theory and practice*, 2nd Edition. Boston, MA: Allyn & Bacon.

Bowen, D.N. & Bowen, E.A. (1992). Multicultural education: The learning style aspect. In Grant, C.A. (Ed.), *Toward education that is multicultural: Proceedings of the first annual meeting of the National Association for Multicultural Education*. Morristown, NJ: Silver Burdett Ginn, 266-276.

Boyer, J.B. (1989). *Collegiate instructional discrimination index. (multiethnic, multilingual, cross-racial, non-sexist)*. Manhattan, KS: Kansas State University, College of Education.

Boyer, J.B. (1990). *Curriculum materials for ethnic diversity*. Lawrence, KS: Center for Black Leadership and Development, University of Kansas.

Boyer, J.B. (1992). Multicultural concerns in educational research. *Midwestern Educational Researcher*, 5 (2), Spring, 7-8.

Boyer, J.B. (1985). *Multicultural education: Product or process* (reprinted 1991). New York: ERIC Center on Urban Education, Teachers College, Columbia University.

Brislin, R.W. (1981). *Cross-cultural encounters: Face-to-face interaction*. Elmsford, NY: Pergamon.

Brislin, R., Cushner, K., Cherries, C., & M. Yong. (1976). *Beyond culture*. New York: Anchor Press.

Brislin, R., Cushner, K., Cherries, C., & M. Yong. (1986). *Intercultural interactions: A practical guide*. Beverly Hills, CA: Sage.

Colangelo, N., Dustin, D., & Foxley, C. (1985). *Multicultural nonsexist education: A human relations approach*. Dubuque, IA: Kendall Hunt.

Coleman, J. (1966). *Equality of educational opportunity*. Washington, DC: Office of Education, U.S. Department of Health, Education and Welfare.

Cortes, C. (1995). Mass media as multicultural curriculum: Public competitor to school education. *Multicultural Education*, 2 (3), Spring, 4-7.

Cross, D., Baker, G., & Styles, L. (1977). *Teaching in a multicultural society: Perspectives and professional strategies*. New York: Free Press.

Cubberly, E. (1909). *Changing conceptions of education.* New York: Riverside Educational Mimeographs.

Cushmer, K. (1992). *Human diversity in education.* New York: McGraw-Hill.

Davidman, L. & Davidman, P.T. (1994). *Teaching with a multicultural perspective: A practical guide.* White Plains, NY: Longman.

Della-Dora, D., *et. al.* (Eds.). (1974). *Education for an open society.* Washington, DC: Association for Supervision and Curriculum Development.

Derman-Sparks, L. (1989). *Anti-bias curriculum. Tools for empowering young children.* Washington DC: National Association for the Education of Young Children.

Fairchild, H.P. (1926). *The melting pot mistake.* Boston, MA: Little, Brown.

Ford, B. (1992). Developing teachers with a multicultural perspective: A challenge and a mission. In Grant, C.A. (Ed.), *Toward education that is multicultural: Proceedings of the first annual meeting of the National Association for Multicultural Education.* Morristown, NJ: Silver Burdett Ginn, 132-138.

Ford, M. (1979). The development of an instrument for assessing levels of ethnicity in public school teachers. Unpublished doctoral dissertation, University of Houston, Houston, TX.

Fuchs, L.H. (1990). *The American kaleidoscope: Race, ethnicity, and the civic culture.* Wesleyan, CT: The University Press of New England.

Garcia, R.L. (1991). *Teaching in a pluralistic society: Concepts, models, strategies.* New York: HarperCollins.

Gardner, H. (1983). *Frames of mind.* New York: Basic Books.

Gay, G. (1994). *At the essence of learning: Multicultural education.* West Lafayette, IN: Kappa Delta Pi.

Gay, G. (1995). Curriculum theory and multicultural education. In Banks, J. & Banks, C. (Eds.), *Handbook of research on multicultural education.* New York: MacMillan Publishing Co., 25-43.

Gay, K. (1987). *The rainbow effect: Interracial families.* New York: Franklin Watts.

Gillie, O. (1977). Did Sir Cyril Burt fake his research on hereditability of intelligence? (Part 1). *Phi Delta Kappan,* February, 469-471.

Gollnick, D.M. & Chinn, P.C. (1994). *Multicultural education in a pluralistic society,* 4th Edition. Columbus, OH: MacMillan.

Good, T.L. (1981). Teacher expectations and student perceptions: A decade of research. *Educational Leadership, 38* (5), 415-422.

Good, T.L. & Brophy, J. (1990). *Educational psychology: A realistic approach,* 4th Edition. New York: Longman.

Gooden, C. (1990). That's a good idea, but.... Unpublished manuscript. Houston, TX: Texas Southern University.

Green, T.F. (1966). *Education and pluralism: Ideal and reality.* Twenty-sixth annual T. Richard Street Lecture, School of Education, Syracuse University, Syracuse, NY.

Hernandez, H. (1989). *Multicultural education.* London, United Kingdom: Merrill.

Hill, H.D. (1989). *Effective stategies for teaching minority students.* Bloomington, IN: National Educational Service.

Hoopes, D.S. & Ventura, P. (1979). *Intercultural sourcebook.* LaGrange Park, IL: Intercultural Network.

Hughes, E.M. (1990). Taking responsiblity for cultural diversity. *Black Issues in*

Higher Education, 24-27.

Jencks, C.S. *et al.* (1972). *Inequality: A reassessment of the effect of family and schooling in America*. New York: Basic Books.

Jensen, A.R. (1969). How much can we boost IQ and scholastic achievement? *Harvard Educational Review*, 39 (1), 1-123.

Kallen, H. (1956). *Cultural pluralism and the American idea*. Philadelphia, PA: University of Philadelphia Press.

Kozol, J. (1991). *Savage inequalities: Children in America's schools*. New York: Crown.

Kraig, G.M. (1992). Implementation of a multicultural education in teacher training program. In Grant, C.A. (Ed.), *Toward education that is multicultural: Proceedings of the first annual meeting of the National Association for Multicultural Education*. Morristown, NJ: Silver Burdett Ginn, 139-147.

Krug, M. (1976). *The melting of the ethnics*. Bloomington, IN: Phi Delta Kappa.

Kunjufu, J. (1984). *Developing positive self-images and discipline in black children*. Chicago, IL: African American Images.

Kunjufu, J. (1985). *Countering the conspiracy to destroy black boys*. Chicago, IL: African American Images.

Kunjufu, J. (1986). *Motivating and preparing black youth to work*. Chicago, IL: Afrikan American Images.

Labelle, T. & Ward, C. (1994). *Multiculturalism and education, diversity and its impact on schools and society*. Albany, NY: State University of New York Press.

Moynihan, D.P. (1965). *The Negro family: The case for national action*. Washington, DC: U.S. Department of Labor.

Myrdal, G. (1962). *An America dilemma: The Negro problem and modern democracy*. New York: Harper & Row.

Nebraska Department of Education. (1993). Rule 16 Approval of school district multicultural education programs. Lincoln, NE: Equal Education Opportunities Section (301 Centennial Mall South, Lincoln, NE 68509).

Novak, M. (1973). *The rise of the unmeltable ethnics*. New York: Macmillan.

Oliver, J.P (1991). The relationship between the racial attitudes of white college freshmen and sophomores as influenced by exposure to multiculturalism in education practices. Unpublished doctoral dissertation, Kansas State University, Manhattan, KS.

Pacheco, A. (1977, May-June). Cultural pluralism: A philosophical analysis. *Journal of Teacher Education*, 16-20.

Palmer, P. (1990). The Courage to Teach and to Learn. A speech given as part of the Chester E. Peters Lecture and Student Development Series, Kansas State University, Manhattan, KS, November 29.

Parsons, T. (1965). Full citizenship for the negro American. In Parsons, T. & Clark, K.B. (Eds), *The Negro American*. Boston, MA: Houghton-Mifflin.

Pine, G.J. & Hilliard, A.G. (1990). Rx for racism: Imperatives for America's schools. *Phi Delta Kappan,* 71 (8), 593-600.

Pratte, R. (1979). *Pluralism in education*. Springfield, IL: Charles C. Thomas.

Pusch, M.D., (Ed.). (1979). *Multicultural education: A cross cultural training approach*. Chicago, IL: Intercultural Press.

Ramsey, P.G., Vold, E.B., & Williams, L.R. (1989). *Multicultural education: A*

Resource book. New York: Garland.

Reed, D.F. (1992). Preparing teachers for multicultural classrooms. In Grant, C.A. (Ed.), *Toward education that is multicultural: Proceedings of the first annual meeting of the National Association for Multicultural Education.* Morristown, NJ: Silver Burdett Ginn.

Reyhner, J. (1988). *Teaching the Indian child* (2nd edition). Billings, MT: Eastern Montana College.

Richard-Amato, P.A. (1988). *Making it happen*. New York: Longman.

Richard-Amato, P.A. & Snow, M.A. (Eds.). (1992). *The multicultural classroom: Readings for content-area teachers*. White Plains, NY: Longman.

Rodgers-Rose, L. (1980). *The Black woman*. London, United Kingdom: Sage.

Rodriguez, F. (1983). *Education in a multicultural society*. Washington DC: University Press of America.

Roosevelt, T. (1910). *Americanism*. [Speech given in 1910].

Scarcella, R. (1992) Providing culturally sensitive feedback. In Richard-Amato, P.A. & Snow, M.A., (Eds.), *The multicultural classroom: Readings for content-area teachers*. White Plains, NY: Longman.

Schaefer, R.T. (1990). *Racial and ethnic groups*. New York: Harper Collins.

Shirts, R.G. 1973. "Bafa Bafa" Simile II. Post Office Box 910, Delman, CA, 92014.

Sizemore, B. (1980). The politics of multicultural education. Unpublished manuscript.

Sleeter, C.E. & Grant, C.A. (1987). An analysis of multicultural education in the United States. *Harvard Educational Review*, 57 (4), 421-39.

Sleeter, C.E. & Grant, C.A. (1988). *Making choices for multicultural education: Five approacxhes to race, class, and gender*. Columbus, OH: Merrill.

Stewart, E.C. (1971). *American cultural patterns: A cross-cultural perspective*. Chicago, IL: Intercultural Press.

Stewart, E.C. (1973). Dimensions in cross cultural instruction. Paper presented at the International Communication Convention, April.

Suzuki, B.H. (1979). Multicultural education: What's it all about? *Integrated Education*, 17, 43-49.

Suzuki, B.H. (1984). Curriculum transformation for multicultural education. *Education and Urban Society*, 11, 294-322.

Willie, C.V. (1987). *Effective education*. Westport, CT: Greenwood.

Willis, S. (1993). Multicultural teaching. *Curriculum Update*, Association for Supervision and Curriculum Development, September.

Witkin, H.A., Moore, C.A., & MacDonald, F.J. (1974). *Cognitive style and theteaching/learning processes*. (Cassette Series 3F). Washington, DC: American Educational Research Association.

Zangwill, I. (1922). *The melting pot: Drama in four acts*. New York: Macmillan. Originally produced in 1908.

Other References

Adler, S. (1993). *Multicultural communication skills in the classroom*. Boston, MA: Allyn & Bacon.

Andereck, M.E. (1992). *Ethnic awareness in the school: An ethnographic study*. Newbury Park, CA: Sage.

Asante, M.K. (1995). *African American history: A journey of liberation*. Maywood, NJ: The People's Publishing Group.

Athanases, S.Z., Christiano, D., & Lay, E. (1995). Fostering empathy and finding common ground in multiethnic classes. *English Journal*, 84 (9), 26.

Atwater, M.M., Radzik-Marsh, K., & Struchens, M. (Eds.). (1994). *Multicultural education: Inclusion of all*. Athens, GA: The University of Georgia-Department of Science Education.

Bachman, J. (1994). Multicultural education: A program to benefit our students and society. *NASSP Bulletin*, 78 (11), 68.

Bailey, S.M. & Campbell, P.B. (1992). Gender equity: The unexamined basic of school reform. *Stanford Law & Policy Review*, 4, 73-86.

Baker, G.C. (1994). *Planning and organizing for multicultural instruction*. Menlo Park, CA: Addison-Wesley.

Banks, J.A. (1993). Multicultural education: Progress and prospects. *Phi Delta Kappan*, 21.

Banks, J.A. (1993). Multicultural education: Development, dimensions, and challenges. *Phi Delta Kappan*, 22-27.

Boyer, J.B. (1990). Barriers and bridges to multicultural education in American schools. In *Accommodating change and diversity: Multicultural practices in rural schools*. New York: Ford Foundation (Ford Western Task Force, Rural Clearinghouse for Lifelong Learning).

Brantlinger, E.A. (1993). *The politics of social class in secondary school: Views of affluent and impoverished youth*. New York: Teachers College Press.

Bull, B.L., Fruehling, R.T., & Chattergy, V. (1992). *The ethics of multicultural and bilingual education*. New York: Teachers College Press.

Burgos-Sassceer, R. (1987). Empowering Hispanic students: A prerequisite is adequate data, *Journal of Education Equity and Leadership*, 7 (1), Spring.

Carpenter, K.D. (1994). Achieving a true multicultural focus in today's curriculum. *NASSP Bulletin*, 78 (6), 62.

DeVilla, R.A., Faltis, C.J., & Cummins, J.P. (Eds.). (1994). *Cultural diversity in schools*. Albany, NY: State University of New York Press.

Diaz-Rico, L. & Weed, K.Z. (1995). *Crosscultural language and academic development handbook*. Boston, MA: Allyn & Bacon.

Edelman, M.W. (1992). *The measure of our success: A letter to my children and yours*. Boston, MA: Beacon Press.

Evertson, C.M. & Weade, R. (1991). The social construction of classroom lessons. In Waxman, H.C. & Walberg, H.J. (Eds.), *Effective teaching, current research*. Berkeley, CA: McCutchan.

Fiske, E.B. (1991). *Smart schools, smart kids*. New York: Simon & Schuster.

Garcia, E. (1995). Educating Mexican American students: Theory, research, policy, and practice. In Banks, J.A. (Ed.), *Handbook of research on multicultural education*. New York: Simon & Schuster MacMillan.

Garcia, J. & Pugh, S.L. (1993). Multicultural education in teacher prepartion programs: A political or an educational concept? *Phi Delta Kappan*, 214-219.

Gonzales, J., Roberts, H., Harris, O.D., Huff, D.J., Johns, A.M., Ray. L., & Scott, O.L. (1994). *Teaching from a multicultural perspective*. Thousand Oaks, CA: Sage.

Grant, C.A. (Ed.) (1992). *Multicultural education for the 21st century: Proceedings of the second annual meeting of The National Association for*

Multicultural Education. Morristown, NJ: Paramount Publishing-Silver Burdett Ginn.

Grant, C.A. (Ed.) (1995). *National Association for Multicultural Education 1993 & 1994 Proceedings*. San Francisco, CA: Caddo Gap Press.

Hale, J.E. (1982). *Black children: Their roots, culture, and learning styles*. Provo, UT: Brigham Young University Press.

Hollins, E.R., King, J.E., & Hayman, W.C. (1994). *Teaching diverse populations*. Albany, NY: State Univeristy of New York Press.

Howard, G.R. (1994). Whites in multicultural education: Rethinking our role. *Phi Delta Kappan*, 36-41.

Jimenez, E. & Lockheed, M.E. (1989). Enhancing girls' learning through single sex education: Evidence and a policy conundrum. *Educational Evaluation and Policy Analysis*, 11, 117-142.

Jones, J.M. (1972). *Prejudice and racism*. Reading, MA: Addison-Wesley.

Jordan C., Tharp, R.G., & Baird-Vogt, L. (1992). Chapter 1. In Saravior-Shon, M. & Arvizu, S. (Eds.), *Cross-cultural literacy: Ethnographies of communication in multiethnic classrooms*. New York: Garland.

Kanpol, B. & McLaren, P. (Eds.). (1995). *Critical multiculturalism: Uncommon voices in a common struggle*. Westport, CT: Bergin & Garvey.

Klein, S.S. (1985). *Handbook for achieving sex equity through education*. Baltimore, MD: The Johns Hopkins University Press.

Klein, S.S. & Ortman, P.E. (1994). Continuing the journey toward gender equity. *Educational Researcher*, 25, 13-21.

Knapp, M. & Shields, P. (Eds.). (1991). *Better schooling for the children of poverty: Alternatives to conventional wisdom*. Berkeley, CA: McCutchan.

Kreidler, W.J. (1995). Say good-bye to bias. *Instructor*, 104 (1), 28.

Kuykendall, C. (1992). *From rage to hope: Strategies for reclaiming Black and Hispanic students*. Bloomington, IN: National Education Service Publishers.

Lee, C. & Slaughter-Defoe, D. (1995). Historical and sociocultural influences on African American education. In Banks, J.A. (Ed.), *Handbook of research on multicultural education*. New York: Simon & Schuster MacMillan.

Lee, V.E. & Marks, H.M. (1992). Who goes where? Choice of single sex and coeducational independent secondary schools. *Sociology of Education*, 65 (3), 226-253

Lockheed, M.E. & Lee, V.E. (1993). Single-sex and coeducational education. *International encyclopedia of education*, 2, 576-580.

Lynch, E.W. & Hanson, M.J. (1992). *Developing cultural competence*. Baltimore, MD: Paul H. Brookes.

Nixon, H.L. & Henry, W.J. (1992). White students at the black university: Their experiences regarding acts of racial intolerance. *Equity and Excellence*, 25 (3), 121.

Pang, V.O. (1994). Why do we need this class? Multicultural education for teachers. *Phi Delta Kappan*, 289-292.

Pang, V.O. (1995). Asia Pacific American students: A diverse and complex population. In Banks, J.A. (Ed.), *Handbook of research on multicultural education*. New York: Simon & Schuster MacMillan.

Parkay, F.W. (1983). *White teacher, black school: The professional growth of a ghetto teacher*. New York: Praeger.

Peters, W. (1987). *A class divided then and now*. New Haven, CT: Yale

Univeristy Press.

Pignatelli, F. & Pflaum, S.W. (1993). *Celebrating diverse voices*. Newbury Park, CA: Corwin Press.

Price, H.B. (1992). Multiculturalism: Myths and realities. *Phi Delta Kappan*, 208-213.

Robinson, B.J. & Shade, C. (Eds.). (1989). *Culture, style, and the educative process*. Springfield, IL: Charles C. Thomas.

Sadker, M.P. & Sadker, D.M. (1982). *Sex equity handbook for school*. New York: Longman.

Sadker, M. & Sadker, D. (1994). *Failing at fairness: How America's schools cheat girls*. New York: Charles Scribner's Sons.

Sergiovanni, T.J. (1992). *Moral leadership: Getting to the heart of school improvement*. San Francisco, CA: Jossey-Bass.

Singer, A. (1994). Reflections on multiculturalism. *Phi Delta Kappan*, 284-288.

Spindler, G. & Spindler, L. (Eds.). (1994). *Pathways to cultural awareness*. Thousand Oaks, CA: Corwin Press.

Spring, J. (1995). *The intersection of cultures: Multicultural education in the United States*. New York: McGraw-Hill.

Tiedt, P.L. & Tiedt, I.M. (1995). *Multicultural teaching: A handbook of activities, information and resources*. Boston, MA: Allyn & Bacon.

Truely, W.G. (1991). The needs of African-American girls. *National NOW Times*, 23 (4), 4.

Tyack, D. & Hansot, E. (1990). *Learning together: A history of coeducation in American public schools*. New Haven, CT: Yale University Press and the Russell Sage Foundation.

Wayman, H., Felix, J., Anderson, J., & Baptiste, Jr., H.P. (1992). *Students at risk in at-risk schools: Improving environments for learning*. Newbury Park, CA:. Corwin Press.

Wheelock, A. (1992). *Cross the tracks: How "untracking" can save America's schools*. New York: The New Press.

Whiting, A.N. (1991). *Guardians of the flame: Historically black colleges yesterday, today, and tomorrow*. Washington, DC: American Association of State Colleges and Universities.

Index

A

academic achievement and ethnic growth, 51-52

academic growth, 59

academic justice, 162-163

academic racism and sexism, 168-169, 207, 209-210

academic research, 205-206

acculturation, defined, 25

Adler, S., 196

Administrator's Checklist for Enhancing Multi-Cultural Curriculum (Boyer), 234-238

administrative competencies for multicultural settings, 244-246

affective competencies, 216

affective domain, 135-136

African American history, literature, and music, 208

African American males and single sex schooling, 220

African American students, 28, 30, 33-34

African Americans

in agricultural education curriculum, 84-85

in arts curriculum, 79-81

in business and technology curriculum, 76-78

in drama/theatre curriculum, 81-82

in elementary education curriculum, 70-71

in English and language curriculum, 67-68

in human ecology curriculum, 74-75

in journalism and mass communication curriculum, 75-76

in library media services, 83-84

in mathematics curriculum, 73-74

in modern language curriculum, 82-83

in music curriculum, 78-79

in science and health curriculum, 71-73

in social studies curriculum, 68-69

and sociological concepts, 19-20

age discrimination, 32-33

agricultural education curriculum, 84-85

American Contrast, 120

Americanism and racism, 19-22

Americanization, 16-17, 22

Americans with Disabilities Act, 32, 36

An American Dilemma (Myrdal), 15

Anglo-Saxon, 16-17, 20-21

Anderson, J.A., 90

Archer, C., 97-98, 114

arts curriculum, 79-81

Asian Americans

in agricultural education curriculum, 84-85

in arts curriculum, 79-81

in business and technology curriculum, 76-78

N

About the Authors

James B. Boyer is a professor of Curriculum & American Ethnic Studies at Kansas State University where he has been active with Multicultural Education Institutes and Doctoral Studies on Curriculum & Cultural Understandings. His most recent research is focused on

African American males in classrooms and the dynamics of cross-racial, cross-ethnic teaching and learning. He has authored or edited *Curriculum Materials for Ethnic Diversity, Teaching the Economically Poor,* and several checklists including the *Collegiate Instructional Discrimination Index* and the *Multicultural Instructional Inventory for Enhancing College-University Curriculum.* He coordinates the urban master's program in curriculum based in Kansas City. Boyer has also served as the Executive Director of the National Association for Multicultural Education.

H. Prentice Baptiste, Jr. is a professor in Foundations and Adult Education and associate director of the Center for Science Education at the College of Education at Kansas State University. His research interests include the conceptualization of multicultural education, the process of multiculturalizing educational entities, and culturally diversifying science and mathematics instruction. Baptiste has authored or edited six books, and numerous articles, papers, and chapters in multicultural education and science education. He works

extensively with urban and rural schools and school districts in designing and implementing comprehensive multicultural plans. He has presented papers and conducted workshops in Egypt, Germany, Jamaica, Morocco, and the Netherlands.

2238